SWIM 30 LAPS IN 30 DAYS

Do not begin this or any other exercise program without first
consulting your physician.

S~W~I~M
30 LAPS
IN 30 DAYS

A World Master's Program for
Swimming Farther, Faster and Better

JANE KATZ, Ed.D.

Illustrated by Michael Brown

A PERIGEE BOOK

Perigee Books
are published by
The Putnam Publishing Group
200 Madison Avenue
New York, NY 10016

W.E.T.s® (Water Exercise Techniques)
is a registered trademark of Jane Katz, Ed.D.
SWEATS to W.E.T.s® ™ is a trademark of Jane Katz, Ed.D.

Library of Congress Cataloging-in-Publication Data

Katz, Jane.
Swim 30 laps in 30 days : a world master's program for swimming
farther, faster, and better / Jane Katz ; illustrated by Michael
Brown.
p.   cm.
1. Swimming.   2. Swimming—Training.   3. Physical fitness.
I. Title.   II. Title: Swim thirty laps in thirty days.
GV837.K354 1991   90-45429 CIP
613.7'16—dc20
ISBN 0-399-51667-0

Cover design © 1991 by Mike McIver
Front cover photograph © by Douglas Kirkland/SYGMA

Printed in the United States of America

3   4   5   6   7   8   9   10

Contents

Acknowledgments

My thanks first, as always, to my parents "The Profs"—Dorothea and Leon—for their enduring enthusiasm in every way, and especially for putting up with me through the decades. But then, what are parents for?

Heartfelt thanks to my siblings and their families, particularly my sister Elaine, as well as my sister June and brother Paul, also Joel and Arden, who have in their turn given me Stevie, Jason, Justin, and Austen David. They have all lent encouragement, caring, given input and supported this book through the pleasure of their presence, especially poolside. And to Ceo for everything.

Among friends and colleagues, my thanks go to Dr. Herbert Erlanger for his patience and caring; to Elaine Fincham, super swimmer, whose sharing is always invaluable; and to Dr. Howard Chislett, whose friendship has stood the test of time.

I am indebted to photographer Douglas Kirkland for his brilliant photography and generosity.

To Gil Rogin, fellow swimming enthusiast and renowned sports authority, my special regard for his timely Foreword.

To Anne Goldstein, typist, a bouquet for her devotion to her work and her flexible hours.

My appreciation to Judy Linden, Senior Editor, Marilyn Ducksworth, Sharon Stahl, Laura Allen, and the staff at Putnam's for their professional guidance and understanding. And to Don Farber and Norman Rosenberg for their expertise. To Michael Brown for bringing his illustrations to water.

To all the students I have taught at Bronx Community College, John Jay College of Criminal Justice, and Borough of Manhattan Community College of the City University of New York, my heartfelt thanks for always proving that water is wonderful and that you can swim better, farther and faster.

I thank the countless swimmers and Masters swimming friends I have met all over the world and congratulate them for their commitment to a lifelong fitness and sports activity.

To the democracy of water,
the great equalizer

Foreword

I didn't learn to swim until I was eleven or twelve. Before that what I did was propel myself by putting one hand in front of the other on a rocky lake bottom in about two feet of leech-ridden water. At the same time I kicked. As I went back and forth I imagined I was a motorboat creating a wake. Small kid, small pleasures. Then one day, suddenly, I was swimming. I recall no intermediate, floundering stage. I was simply, amazingly, swimming. An equivalent experience today would be if I had been flapping my arms for years and, all at once, I was flying.

Swimming surely is the closest thing to flying. You've left the careworn earth, your own two feet, of which so much is made. Instead you're stretched out on your stomach, your back, your side as if in carefree sleep, buoyed by this luscious medium, blissed out on the little smacking, licking, chuckling noises of your progress. Moreover, as I keep telling people, done right, swimming is as easy as walking and you feel a whole lot better when you stop and the endorphins kick in. Another good thing about swimming is that it's real tough to get injured. In fact, about the only shortcoming to swimming is the view. The bottom of the pool isn't usually very scenic. But then swimming is inducive to reflection, even daydreaming, so the interior view can be compensating.

Jane has coached me in swimming, and although I may have been more advanced than some, I can vouch for the fact that what she tells you on the following pages really works. Jane Katz's 30-lap goal program in this book keeps you focused.

Gilbert Rogin
Former Managing Editor, *Sports Illustrated*
Corporate Editor, Time Inc. Magazine Co.

Introduction

On a Personal Note

When I began swimming as a youngster, recreation as well as competition was my personal goal. Swimming always was a family affair, and I had total support from my parents.

Regardless of the season, Papa Katz, Mama Katz and the four Katz children trooped off to one of the free New York City Parks Department facilities for their daily dip in the neighborhood "watering hole." The outdoor pool was our "country club" in the city during the summer, where we splashed, lapped, sunned, snacked and had fun among ourselves and with the "locals." We were the epitome of the expression "the family that plays together stays together."

It was in the early fifties that my father, Leon Katz (a swimming buff since the age of fourteen when he was saved from drowning), embarked himself and his family on a course of lifelong fitness through swimming, at a time when fitness was understood to mean rigorous training for sports competition.

Today, physical fitness should be for everyone. Programs ranging from mild to more vigorous exercise are available to anyone who wishes to undertake one. It is a prescription for health and quality of life. Schools, health clubs, community recreation centers, spas, Y's, aquatic facilities offer a variety of fitness activities.

I have been teaching in the City University of New York (CUNY) system since 1964, primarily at Bronx Community College and more recently at John Jay College of Criminal Justice. The student body at these colleges ranges in age from eighteen to eighty, and includes all ethnic backgrounds. They come to swimming on different levels of ability—including nonswimmers, people who swim occasionally but who have developed bad habits along the way, as well as recreational lap swimmers. Nevertheless, these diverse student groups, which also embrace those with special needs, learn fast, have fun, and condition themselves to being in water, as they practice familiar land-based exercises within the confines of the pool. These exercises turn into the drills which become the skills for learning to swim laps as a lifetime fitness activity.

In 1979, I sustained severe injuries in a car accident. My rehabilitation led me to explore innovative body movement techniques in the water to help me restore myself to health. This was how my concept of W.E.T.s® (Water Exercise Techniques) was born; W.E.T.s are land-based exercises which are adapted to the water, or as I say in this book—from "SWEATS to W.E.T.s® ™"

The unique focus of this book is the use of Water Exercise Techniques as drills that are "swim skill specific." These will help you swim laps progressively better, faster and further.

From the broad base of water exercise which everyone can do, through the levels of lap swimming for fitness as well as triathlons and Masters competitions, you can reach your goal with this structured program to *Swim 30 Laps in 30 Days*.

So take the plunge into the wonder world of water!

Jane Katz

Praise for Dr. Jane Katz!

"Follow her book and Dr. Jane Katz will make good on the title. *Swim 30 Laps in 30 Days* can put a few years on your life."
—Jimmy Breslin

"Dr. Jane Katz is the aquatic heroine of modern times."
—Joe Franklin

"Dr. Jane Katz, internationally known fitness expert, has made vast contributions to the world of aquatics through her impact as author, educator, competitor and instructor. Jane's expertise and experiences have earned her the position of Board of Director of the International Swimming Hall of Fame, Inc."
—Samuel James Freas, Ed.D.
President, International Swimming
Hall of Fame, Inc.

"[Dr. Jane Katz has] a gift of being able to get individuals of all ages and descriptions to relax and come to know the water 'as a friend,' a wonderful 'playground,' and a way to add quality to life. . . . A hearty 'Well Done'!"
—John Butterfield, Executive Director
The President's Council on Physical Fitness
and Sports

"Dr. Jane Katz has been blazing new fitness trails for many years, in water and out. She is one of America's most dynamic, skilled and articulate fitness leaders today."
—Joseph E. Curtis, Past President
American Park and Recreation Society

"Dr. Jane Katz's aquatic program is . . . outstanding."
—Thomas R. Collingwood, Ph.D.
Program Services Director
Institute for Aerobics Research

". . . my kudos to Dr. Katz. She really knows how to make even the timid woman a water exercise believer. . . . A wonderful book."
> —Jean L. Fourcroy, M.D., Ph.D.
> President
> National Council on Women in Medicine

"Dr. Jane Katz is a body genius. She helps a dog-paddle klutz like me learn to swim well enough to enjoy it and stay with it enough to get the good it can give."
> —T. George Harris
> Founding Editor
> *American Health* and *Psychology Today*

"I feel the landmark work that [Dr. Jane Katz has] done in teaching people to swim has made a significant national contribution to health and physical fitness."
> —John O. Marsh, Jr.
> Former Secretary of the Army

"Dr. Jane Katz has done for swimming what Dr. Kenneth Cooper has done for aerobics."
> —Suzanne P. Timken
> Vice Chairman, The President's
> Council on Physical Fitness and Sports
> —W. R. Timken, Jr.
> National Masters Swimming Champion

"You are something else. How I admire you."
> —Eleanor Holm
> Olympic Gold Medalist
> 1932 Olympic Swim Team

"Dr. Jane Katz's program and the healing powers of water therapy really work."
> —Major Willie P. Davenport
> Olympic Gold Medalist
> 1968 Track and Field Competition

CHAPTER ~ 1

The Magic of Water

According to the President's Council on Physical Fitness and Sports, people who are physically fit generally enjoy a happier, healthier, and more productive life. Medical research has confirmed that a consistent and enjoyable fitness program can prolong and enhance the quality of your life.

In water, you'll find the ideal enjoyable fitness program. In fact, swimming is one of America's most popular activities especially in warm weather. And why? Because water is magic! It's buoyant. It's resistant. It's aerobic. It's soothing. It's refreshing. It's sensuous. It's mentally restorative. It's fitness and fun!

WHY THIS BOOK

Nevertheless, how often have you heard or even said:

"I can swim, but I can't breathe,"

or

"I can finish one fast lap and then I'm winded,"

or

You are a "self-taught" swimmer and carry a burden of bad habits.

or

You are a product of the "sink or swim" method, and now are reluctant to go near the water.

Swim 30 Laps in 30 Days is a structured program which will teach you to swim farther, faster and better. It is for new, occasional, and seasonal swimmers. It is also for those who swim regularly but have hit a plateau, or have a lifetime of inefficient swim habits.

Part of this program uses specially designed Water Exercise Techniques (W.E.T.s®) that transfer land-based movement to the water to increase and refine your swimming skills. The program progresses from 1 lap to 30 laps. Each new "day" you add another lap, as well as learn new swim skills, W.E.T. drills, and improve your physical conditioning.

This program, however, is not a quick fix! A "day" is defined as being that amount of time it will take you to learn and master the lesson of the "day," before you go on to the next one.

WHY WATER WORKS: SCIENTIFIC SWIM SMARTS

The magic of water has a scientific basis. The specific gravity of water is 1.0. When a body is submerged, the volume of water displaced is equal to the volume of the body being submerged, and pressure is exerted on the body from all sides. Because the specific gravity of your body in water is less than 1.0, you do not sink, but float. Generally women, because they have more adipose (fatty) tissue, float easier than men, who have heavier bones and muscles.

This principle of buoyancy is known as Archimedes' Law, which means that your apparent body weight in chin-deep water is 10 percent of your true weight on land; e.g., if you weigh 150 pounds on land, in the water you weigh only 15! That's a big plus already!

Also, that's why those who cannot exercise on land because they are overweight, have back problems, arthritis, osteoporosis, sports-related injuries, and special needs can exercise and move in water without the stress on joints and muscles of land-based exercise. Swimming is frequently prescribed by physical therapists and sports-medicine specialists, because it develops all the main muscle groups and builds endurance by going the distance. Water is a forgiving medium. Its Lucite cover graciously envelops the body and encourages those who are embarrassed to exercise on land.

Upward, Onward and Forward

Another scientific principle applicable to swimming is Newton's Third Law of Motion, which explains how a body moves forward. It states that for every action there is an equal and opposite reaction. When you are in water and want to go forward, you must push water backward. This is demonstrated in the pulling component of each swim stroke. By moving forward in and through the water you are using muscles and expending energy, similar to a dry-land workout, but in a low-impact, refreshing medium.

This engages your cardiovascular system in aerobic conditioning, improving heart, lungs, and muscles while achieving laps and distance.

Streamlined Swimming

Another principle applicable to swimming is Bernoulli's Principle, or Lift Law, which states in essence that the higher you ride in the water, the faster you go, and vice versa. This is the importance of streamlining your body position because it reduces its resistance in the water, enhances forward propulsion, and increases the distance you can swim by consistently adding laps to your workout.

Speaking of a Lift!

The tranquilizing effect of swimming lap after lap, surrendering your mind to the rhythmic pace of your body riding through the water, and the pleasure of the water washing over you, is an immeasurable benefit toward calming the nerves, refreshing the mind, and restoring your sense of well-being.

The "high" of spirit and energized feeling you enjoy as the result of a workout has its base in the chemical changes which increased exertion and expenditure of energy causes. Your heart and lungs work harder. Oxygen circulates more rapidly through your system carrying away waste products (lactic acid) from your muscles, and your brain begins releasing endorphins—the hormone which acts as a mood elevator and pain blocker.

The stresses of the day get washed away in the soothing waters, where you shut out the rest of the world and can't hear the telephone ring.

At the end of the workout you feel cleansed, toned, euphoric, well rewarded for honoring the commitment you made to yourself to accomplish this swim program.

THE TRAINING EFFECT

This 30-day training program is based on the same principle by which any athlete trains; i.e., gradually increasing the "workload" as you attain increased endurance, strength, flexibility, range of motion, skill, and speed.

This is known as "the training effect," which means putting a bit more demand on yourself than your body can handle comfortably at a given time until it adjusts to the extra "workload" through its increased capacity.

Implementing the "workload" concept is the F. I. T. principle: a gradual increase in Frequency, Intensity, and Time.

WORKOUT COMPONENTS

A workout begins at the beginning, which means you should follow its structure of a Warm-up, Main Set, and a Cool-down.

Warm-up

For five minutes you do a series of land-based exercises transferred to the water: SWEATS to W.E.T.s. They are familiar movements which everyone can do. You carefully warm up the muscles, ease the joints, then stretch, and start to increase the efficiency of your cardiovascular system. You are preparing your body for learning new skills and swimming laps.

Main Set: W.E.T. Drills to Swim Skills

The main set is the central part of your workout—the meat and potatoes. Of the total workout time it is the longest, ranging from 15 to 35 minutes depending on your progress level. It is also that part of your workout where you will swim the longest distance—up to one half mile by the end of this 30-day program.

Cool-down

The cool-down is five minutes of exercises selected from your SWEATS to W.E.T.s which help your body slow down and gradually return to its resting state.

Pump Up the Volume—Check Your Body

You can measure the aerobic effectiveness of your swim workout by checking your pulse rate at warm-up, main set, and cool-down phases as shown in the Anatomy of a Workout. You will find your heart or pulse rate increasing during your main set. To find your target heart rate use the following formula:

Determine your maximum heart rate (MHR) by subtracting your age from 220. Your Target Heart Rate (THR) is 60 percent to 80 percent of your MHR. This should be your heart rate during your main set. Your warm-up and cool-down heart rates should be similar to each other.

Take your pulse by counting the beats at your wrist or on either side of your neck at your carotid artery for six seconds and multiply that count by 10 by adding a zero to that number.

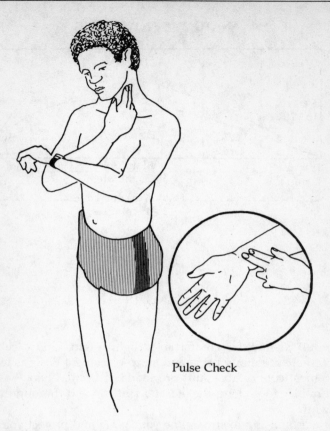

Pulse Check

Recent studies indicate that THRs tend to be 10 percent to 15 percent lower when exercising in water as opposed to exercising on land. You perspire in water, but it gives you an "air-conditioning" benefit so you don't overheat. Therefore, you expend less energy to overcome the heat and are able to exercise more efficiently than on land. The energy you would otherwise use to overcome the heat is used for a more productive workout and increased laps.

With increased physical conditioning, your resting heart rate will become lower than its pre-fitness rate. This is because your heart—itself a muscle—becomes stronger and works more efficiently through the training effect. It pumps more blood, and your cells receive more oxygen with less effort from the heart. This is why being physically fit is so important from a medical/health standpoint and explains why you feel so much better when you are in condition.

ANATOMY OF A WORKOUT

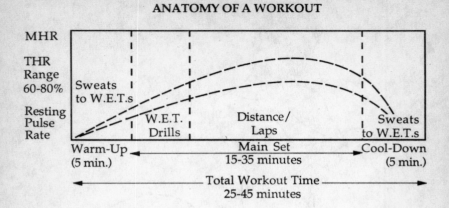

GEARING UP

Suit Up

A *swimsuit* should be comfortable, lightweight, and sleek. For women, there are many back- and strap-placement designs for best fit. The most comfortable suits are made of Lycra. Nylon suits are most durable. To prolong the life of a suit, rinse it thoroughly after each swim.

Wear a *bathing cap* to streamline your body and protect your hair. Choose a snug-fitting bathing cap made from latex rubber, Lycra, or silicone which covers your ears.

Goggles improve your underwater vision (there's a whole new universe underwater!) and enhance your workout. There are a number of features in goggle design which should be considered when purchasing a pair. Among them are tint (light for indoor, dark for outdoor), nosepiece, strap placement, antifog, foam cushioning, and peripheral vision. The shape of your face will influence your choice of goggles for comfort and fit.

If you wear *contact lenses* when swimming, then goggles are a necessity to protect your eyes and lenses and keep them water free. Prescription lens goggles are also available.

A *waterproof watch* that indicates seconds (a visible sweep-second hand), as well as minutes, is desirable.

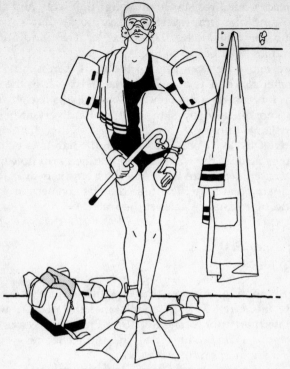

The Totally Equipped Swimmer

Poolside Accessories

The following "swim toys" are usually available poolside and are provided by the facility. If you have a backyard pool, you may want to obtain some of this equipment.

A *kickboard* is standard equipment used for practicing certain Drills to Skills, as well as for kicking in your workout. Kickboards are made of high-density Styrofoam.

A *pull-buoy* is usually made of two Styrofoam cylinders held together by two cords or straps which can be stretched so that the cylinders part, allowing them to be placed high between the legs for support so that you can work on your arm strokes. The pull-buoy is used primarily when learning a new stroke or for building upper-body strength. The larger the buoy, the more buoyancy it provides.

Another popular "swim toy" is *fins*. They slip onto your feet like shoes and cause your legs to move a lot of water. When you kick with fins, you place added resistance on your thigh, calf, and abdominal muscles. Using fins improves your cardiovascular capacity and makes your feet and ankles more flexible. They add variety to a workout and are a lot of fun to use.

There are many kinds of fins on the market in a range of sizes, shapes, materials, and textures. The latest splash is the monofin, where both foot inserts are on one fin which looks like a fishtail. The mask and snorkel used by skin- and scuba-divers are sometimes adopted by lap swimmers.

Hand paddles and web gloves are worn on the hands to help increase the resistance against the water and strengthen arm power.

Water exercise gear. There are numerous products available in the aquatic industry that help maximize the effectiveness of water exercises by adding resistance against the water.

Grooming Amenities

Your Skin

If you are swimming outdoors, the exposure to sun and water calls for definite measures to keep your skin moist. Use a waterproof sunscreen with an appropriate SPF (Sun Protection Factor). Keep in mind that your skin is subject to the ultraviolet rays of the sun whether you are in or out of the water.

After your workout, shower, towel dry, and then apply your favorite skin moisturizer to help replace the loss of your skin's natural moisture.

Your Hair

Before your swim, apply your favorite conditioner to your hair tips. For added protection use a Lycra cap under a latex cap to help keep your hair in place and dry. Shower and shampoo after each swim and apply conditioner occasionally.

Your Ears

For added protection place a small piece of lamb's wool which can be coated with petroleum jelly in each ear and hold securely with the cap over your ears. Towel your ears gently to remove any excess water after your workout. If needed, moisten a cotton swab with rubbing alcohol and dab the ear gently to hasten water evaporation.

FOR SAFETY'S SAKE

Before starting this or any exercise program, have a medical checkup.
No matter what, water safety comes first.

Never swim alone. Be sure to be in a supervised area with a lifeguard on duty. Swim in a depth of water that is safe and comfortable according to your ability. Look for pool markers and dividers, especially when swimming in an unfamiliar pool.

In an open-water area, check for any obstacles and depth.

Follow this program slowly. Your physical condition should indicate your workout progress.

Listen to your body. It will tell you whether you are energized or fatigued.

Always warm up before your main set and cool down afterward.

Read and observe posted safety signs whether you swim at the Y, neighborhood recreation center, health club, when traveling, or even in a backyard pool.

For your own information, learn the ABCs of CPR (Cardio-Pulmonary Resuscitation). Call your local American Red Cross chapter, the American Heart Association or the American Medical Association for courses near you.

HOW THIS PROGRAM WORKS

Once again, remember, this program is not a quick fix! A "Day" is defined as being whatever amount of time it will take you to learn and master the lesson of the day before you go on to the next Day.

The swim workouts of the program are constructed on the F.I.T. Principle, a gradual increase in Frequency, Intensity and Time. It offers both the beginning swimmer and the fitness swimmer the incentive to develop swim skill efficiency, endurance, increasing speed through laps and distance. This "training effect" is built into the program.

The program in *Swim 30 Laps in 30 Days* is made up of five levels of increasing difficulty.

- Each level introduces a new swim stroke.
- Each level has six steps or Days.
- Each level advances to the next level every six Days.
- Each level includes W.E.T. drills, swim skills, and incremental lap increases. W.E.T. drills are the exercises that help develop your swim techniques.
- Each level increases the time and distance you swim.

The program is structured on the following format:

- Each day, beginning with Day 1, you will learn skills via W.E.T. drills which build your laps and distance.
- Each day you will increase your distance by adding another lap or 25 yards. One lap is equal to 25 yards. Adjust the number of laps for pools of different lengths.
- Each day details the basic swim skills for your workout.
- Each day's workout has a structured warm-up, main set, and cool-down.

Each warm-up and cool-down remains constant at five minutes.

In each succeeding level, the main set increases by five minutes, progressing from a 15-minute workout at Level 1 to 35 minutes at Level 5.

The cumulative distance and time in the main set of your workout is a combination of W.E.T. drills and laps for distance. Stay on each Day's workout until you are comfortable and ready for the next one.

There are two "timed" swims in each level to measure your progress swimming laps faster and farther.

Ideally, you should work out three times a week on alternate days. If you progress to the next day each swim, you can complete the program in 10 weeks.

Working out twice a week, you can complete the program in 15 weeks. Working out once a week, you can complete the program in 30 weeks.

To bring your workout poolside, write it on a 3×5 index card or piece of paper with a ballpoint pen. Wet the paper and place it on the deck where it will adhere, and you can refer to it conveniently as you do your workout and laps.

Look for the "Swim Tip" included with each workout "Day." For example:

> *Swim Tip*: Stay on each Day until you have mastered the skills and laps for that Day, before going on to the next Day.

By the end of the *30 Laps in 30 Days* program you will be swimming approximately one-half mile in a 45-minute workout.

The "30 Laps in 30 Days Program Chart" highlights the program.

30 Laps in 30 Days Program Chart

Level	Day	Laps/ 25 yds	Highlighted Strokes	Main Set Time in min.	Workout Total Time in min.	Total Distance in Yds
I	1	1		15	25	25
	2	2		15	25	50
	3	3		15	25	75
	4	4	CRAWL STROKE	15	25	100
	5	5		15	25	125
	6	6		15	25	150
II	7	7		20	30	175
	8	8	ELEMENTARY	20	30	200
	9	9	AND	20	30	225
	10	10	WINDMILL	20	30	250
	11	11	BACKSTROKE	20	30	275
	12	12		20	30	300
III	13	13		25	35	325
	14	14		25	35	350
	15	15	BREASTSTROKE	25	35	375
	16	16	AND	25	35	400
	17	17	FREESTYLE	25	35	425
	18	18		25	35	450
	19	19		30	40	475
	20	20		30	40	500
	21	21		30	40	525
	22	22	SIDESTROKE	30	40	550
	23	23		30	40	575
	24	24		30	40	600
V	25	25		35	45	625
	26	26		35	45	650
	27	27		35	45	675
	28	28	BUTTERFLY	35	45	700
	29	29		35	45	725
	30	30		35	45	750–850

See Appendix B, the "Stroke Checklist Charts," for tips to overcome common faulty swim habits.

C H A P T E R ~ 2

The 30-Day Program

What's Wrong with This Picture?

Coney Island Crawler

BREATHING IS BASIC!

Coney Island does exist. It's a beach on the Atlantic Ocean in Brooklyn, New York. The illustration depicts a likeness of swimming, which might be the crawl stroke. The swimmer is thrashing from side to side in an effort to get enough air, his legs are sinking, his arms are churning, and he's going nowhere fast. He is showing off while exhausting himself. No doubt you've seen his clone at your local beach or pool. The main problem with our "Coney Island Crawler" is that he doesn't know how to breathe and he is wasting too much energy swimming.

Getting the oxygen your body needs in the most efficient way possible is the key to good swimming. Proper breathing removes the lactic acid and other waste products from your body. When you exhale, carbon dioxide is removed from your system; when you inhale, fresh oxygen becomes available to supply your muscles for their continued work. If you're not doing this, you're creating an "oxygen debt" and it acts the same in your body as it would in your checkbook. You wouldn't be able to keep going like that.

Your aim is to make breathing as regular and automatic in swimming as it is out of water. Here are some basic things to remember:

1. *Breathe! Don't overlook the obvious.* It's very simple—you inhale when your face is out of the water, and you exhale and form bubbles when your face is in the water. Some swimmers forget to exhale while their faces are in the water. The point is to breathe regularly and continuously and *never hold your breath*!
2. *Breathe deeply.* You should inhale fully and exhale fully during each breathing cycle, so that you obtain sufficient oxygen and avoid carbon dioxide buildup.
3. *Use both your nose and mouth.* When you're inhaling, suck air into your mouth as if you were using a straw, and at the same time inhale through your nose as if taking in the fragrance of a flower. When you're exhaling, blow out through your mouth as if you're cooling off hot food and simultaneously expel air through your nose as if you're sneezing.
4. *Practice correct breathing technique.* The coordination of your breathing with your head movement during each stroke is *vitally important* to making swimming enjoyable and productive. Breathing continuously (inhaling and exhaling) is the key to comfort as a swimmer. If these skills aren't coming easily to you, keep practicing and resist the temptation to "cut corners"— you'll pay for it later! This is especially true for the rhythmic breathing technique used in the crawl stroke.

Obviously, *never* inhale under the water!

WARM-UPS AND COOL-DOWNS

Every workout in *Swim 30 Laps in 30 Days* begins with a warm-up and ends with a cool-down. The following 10 SWEATS TO W.E.T.s transfer land-based movements to water, preparing your upper, middle, and lower body muscles for the main set of your workout. Warm up for five minutes doing the muscular warm-ups first (e.g., water walk/jog) and then the stretching exercises. After your main set, stretch out and cool down for five minutes by doing various combinations of SWEATS to W.E.T.s. Hold stretch positions briefly before changing sides.

All W.E.T. exercises should be done in chest- to chin-deep water, except where noted. *And never skip your warm-up!*

SWEATS TO W.E.T.S

1. Water Walking/Jogging: Water walking/jogging immediately adjusts your body to the temperature of the water and its resistance, helping you to warm up.

Standing in chest-deep water, walk, then jog through the water forward, backward, diagonally, and in a circle. You can also "bob" in place, with a half-knee bend.

Move your arms back and forth in a pumping action underwater, coordinating them with your walk or jog, as if you were on land.

Water Walking/Jogging

2. **Head Turns:** Head turns warm up and relax your neck muscles.
   - Tip your head from one side to the other, keeping your ear in line with your shoulder.
   - Lower your chin to your chest and describe a semicircle with your head by rolling it on your chest from one shoulder to the other.
   - Looking straight ahead, pivot your head to the right over your right shoulder, and hold. Repeat to the left. This pivoting action is preparation for rhythmic breathing, in order to swim the crawl stroke properly.

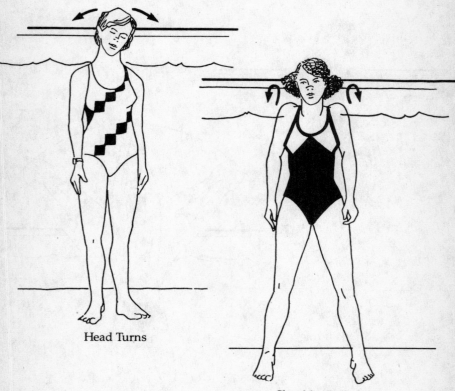

Head Turns

Shoulder Rolls

3. **Shoulder Rolls:** Shoulder rolls warm up and loosen your shoulder area to help increase your range of motion.

With arms relaxed at your sides, lift both shoulders up toward your ears. Roll them backward, then forward several times. Alternately lift and roll each shoulder separately backward and forward.

4. Trunk Turns: Trunk turns warm up midriff muscles and help increase midbody flexibility.

With hands on hips, twist your body at the waist to one side as you inhale. Exhale as you return to the center position. Inhale and turn to the opposite side.

5. Overhead Extension: This warm-up develops a good streamlined body position.

Extend your arms overhead, upper arms covering your ears, elbows straight, thumbs touching. Slowly stretch from side to side at the waist, keeping your arms straight throughout.

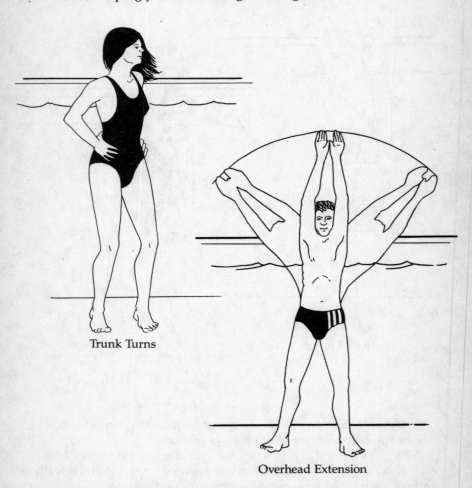

Trunk Turns

Overhead Extension

Tricep Stretch

Cross-Chest Stretch

6. Tricep Stretch: The tricep stretch, a popular swimmer's stretch, helps to limber the upper arm and shoulder area. Extend your left arm over your head, palm facing in. Grasp your left elbow with your right hand, bending it and guiding the left arm to reach behind your head, resting your hand at the base of your neck. Gently pull on the left elbow for additional stretch. Release and reverse arms.

7. Cross-Chest Stretch: This exercise, also a common swimmer's stretch, helps to loosen your back, upper arm and shoulder muscles.

Extend your right arm in front of your body, with thumb pointing up. With your left hand, grasp your right arm underneath the elbow and bring it across your chest under your chin. Repeat with the other arm.

Arm and Leg Stretch

8. Arm and Leg Stretch: This is an overall stretch for general body conditioning.

Stand by the wall in waist-deep water and grasp the pool edge with your right hand. If you can, raise your right foot up to rest on the edge, in front of your hand. Otherwise, place your right foot at a lower point on the wall for a comfortable extension. Reach with your left arm overhead in an arc toward your right side. Hold the stretch, return to your starting position, and reverse.

9. Runners Leg Stretch: This exercise stretches the large muscles of the legs, e.g., the back of the leg, the calf, and the front thigh muscles. These are the muscles most vulnerable to cramping.

Hold the edge of the pool ledge with your left hand. Place the right foot straight behind you, heel touching the bottom of the pool. Bend the left knee and lean forward while stretching the extended leg. Change leg positions and repeat.

Holding on to the pool edge for support, lift your right leg and bend it behind you as if folding it against your body. Grasp your right foot with your right hand, and pull the foot toward your right buttock. Release your foot to a standing position. Repeat on the left side.

Runners' Leg Stretch

Aqua Lunge

10. Aqua Lunge: This exercise helps to increase the range of motion in the hips, and is also excellent as an inner and outer leg stretch.

Face the pool wall and hold the edge with both hands, shoulder width apart. Place your feet against the wall in a straddle position, beyond shoulder width. Shift your body weight to the right, bending the right knee, while the left leg is extended. Hold the stretch. Return to center and shift your body weight to the left.

STROKE COMPONENTS

One of the major differences in swimming strokes is the movement pattern of the arms and legs. They are either alternating or simultaneous. The alternating strokes are the crawl/freestyle and the windmill backstroke. The simultaneous strokes are the elementary backstroke, breaststroke and butterfly. A variation of both stroke patterns is the sidestroke.

The components of any stroke are:

- a streamlined body position—float, glide, and recovery
- the arm motion—catch, pull, and recovery
- the leg motion or kick
- breathing and coordination

The key to correct swimming is a streamlined body position with an efficient stroke technique. This enables you to swim smoothly, gain momentum, and ride high in the water. The foundation for this is the correct floating position.

THE PROGRAM

Level 1

Level 1 teaches and reviews the crawl stroke. It is the fastest and most efficient of all the strokes. Even though there are several other strokes, the crawl stroke is the one most commonly used for recreational, fitness and lap swimming.

Each day in Level 1 has a total workout time of 25 minutes. This includes your five-minute warm-up, a 15-minute main set of W.E.T. drills and laps, and finishes with a five-minute cool-down. Each workout in Level 1 has an optional one minute of kicking practice.

In the Day 1 workout you will swim one lap, or an equivalent distance of 25 yards. Each day builds toward increased distance. In Level 1 you will progress from Day 1 with one lap (25 yards) to Day 6 with six laps (150 yards), so you'll increase with one lap or 25 yards with each day. If on any day you'd like to swim more laps than indicated, just repeat your main set. To chart your progress see page 139.

You will learn the following skills in each day of Level 1. They can be done in chest-deep water.

Level 1

Day	Swim Skills
1	Underwater exhalation (breathing)
	Face float, glide and recover
	Flutter kick
2	Crawl arm stroke
	Crawl arm stroke with flutter kick
	Rhythmic breathing
	Rhythmic breathing with crawl arm stroke
3	Crawl stroke—arms, legs, and rhythmic breathing
	Reading the clock and pulse check
4	Open turn
5	Splashback arm stroke
6	Wide hand entry
	High elbow recovery
	Timed swim and pulse check—1 lap

LEVEL 1   **DAY 1**

SKILLS: Underwater Exhalation (Breathing)
              Face Float, Glide and Recovery
              Flutter Kick

Underwater Exhalation (Breathing)

Stand in chest-deep water and inhale deeply. Slowly exhale the air in a steady stream through your nose and pursed lips. Release the air as continuously and as fully as possible. As you exhale, lower your face into the water and feel the bubbles which your exhalation creates. Exhaling through your nose prevents water from entering the nasal passages. Lift your face out of the water to inhale and repeat the sequence. This is the secret of "breathing underwater," and accustoms you to swimming with your face in the water.

W.E.T. Drill

• *Bobbing and Breathing:* While holding on to the pool wall for support, inhale with your face out of the water. Then begin to exhale while bending your knees so that you are exhaling as you are submerging your face underwater. Continue to exhale through your nose and mouth, forming bubbles. Straighten your knees to a stand and bring your face out of the water. This "bobbing" W.E.T. drill can also be used to relax between laps.

Bobbing and Breathing

Face Float, Glide and Recovery

Assume the overhead stretch position with your arms covering your ears, thumbs together, and bend forward from the waist. Inhale and at the same time bend your knees and push off from the bottom of the pool with the balls of your feet. As you lower your face into the water to forehead level, begin exhaling and straighten your legs behind you to assume a face float streamlined body position.

To recover to a stand, simultaneously bend knees, press arms downward at the sides, lift your head, and place both feet on the bottom. If you are a new floater, practice the recovery to a stand first.

Face Float

Recover to a Stand

W.E.T. Drills

- *Rope Jump:* Simulate jumping rope. As your arms bring the "rope" forward, bend your knees and lift legs to clear "rope." Continue jumping with your head lifting upward as "rope" arcs overhead.
- *Push-off Glide to the Wall:* To glide, face the wall just beyond arm's length distance, with one leg placed in front of the other. Inhale and push off the bottom of the pool by bending your knees, putting your face in the water, and extending your arms so that they are touching your ears. Straighten your legs to a streamlined body position and glide to the pool wall.
- *Push-off Glide from the Wall:* Stand with your back to the wall with one foot against it, bent at the knee. Push off from the wall with both feet, extending body forward on the surface with face in the water. As the glide loses the momentum from your push-off, recover to stand.

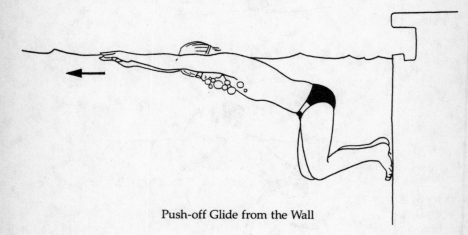

Push-off Glide from the Wall

Flutter Kick

The flutter kick is the leg action for the crawl stroke. It provides balance and propulsion. Your legs move up and down in a continuous alternating movement with the power originating from the hip and thigh muscles. Your knees should be slightly flexed. Keep your ankles loose, and your feet turned slightly inward with big toes brushing in passing.

Flutter Kick

A kickboard is often used both as a support and as training equipment to practice the flutter kick. Hold the kickboard at its rounded end, fingers curling around the edges, and rest your arms on the board at its outer edges. The kickboard will help support you in a floating position, allowing you to practice your flutter kick away from the wall.

W.E.T. Drills
- *Leg Change:* Stand with one leg forward, the other back. Jump with a switch of leg positions, brushing big toes at height of the jump.
- *Wall Flutter Kick:* Hold on to the wall in front float position and flutter kick. Legs should stay underwater, barely breaking surface, making water "boil."

DAY 1 WORKOUT

Distance: 1 lap (25 yards)
Total Time: 25 minutes

Warm-up with SWEATS to W.E.T.s (5 minutes)

Main Set (15 minutes)

  W.E.T. Drills
    Bobbing and Breathing
    Jump Rope
    Push Off Glide to the Wall
    Leg Change
    Wall Flutter Kick

  Distance: 1 lap
    $\frac{1}{2}$ lap Face float, glide, flutter kick and recover from the wall
    $\frac{1}{2}$ lap Flutter kick with kickboard

Cool-down with SWEATS to W.E.T.s (5 minutes)

SWIM TIP: Wearing goggles allows you to keep your eyes open to see where you're going. Underwater, never hold your breath. Exhale continuously.

LEVEL 1   **DAY 2**

SKILLS: Crawl Arm Stroke
Crawl Arm Stroke with Flutter Kick
Rhythmic Breathing
Rhythmic Breathing with Crawl Arm Stroke

Crawl Arm Stroke

Most of the power for the crawl stroke comes from the arm motion, which is divided into three parts: the *catch*, the *pull* and the *recovery*.

The *catch* occurs just after the hand enters the water with a glide. Keeping your hand relaxed and your palm turned slightly outward, with your thumb down straighten your arm at the elbow as your hand catches the water so that it is about eight inches below the water's surface.

The *pull* propels your body forward because you are moving the water backward. With fingers pointed downward, the arm pushes water straight downward and backward with your thumb brushing past your thigh.

The *recovery* returns your arm above the water back to the catch position by bending your elbow and lifting your hand out of the water.

Always keep your elbow higher than your hand throughout the crawl arm stroke motion.

Crawl Armstroke Components

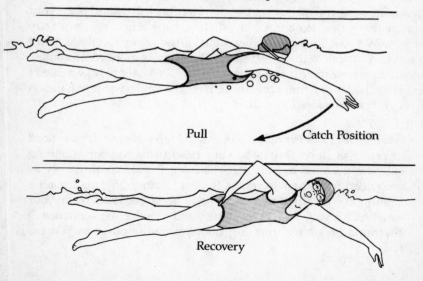

Pull   Catch Position

Recovery

W.E.T. Drill
- *Wall Stroke:* Stand facing pool wall, placing both hands on the edge. With your right arm, start from catch position, pull straight down, touching the side of your leg for the pull. Recover by bending elbow, keeping it higher than your hand, and reach forward toward the wall. Then repeat with left arm.

Crawl Arm Stroke with Flutter Kick

This is the combining of arm and leg components of the crawl stroke. From a face float position, begin a continuous flutter kicking action. Then add the alternating crawl arm stroke, one cycle at a time, keeping your face under water and exhaling. A crawl arm stroke cycle consists of one right-arm pull and one left-arm pull. Stop, take a break, and continue as before.

W.E.T. Drills
- *Crawl Walk:* Using the alternating crawl arm stroke motion, walk forward through chest-deep water. Do this first with your face out of the water and then repeat with your face in the water.
- *Arm and Leg Power:* Use your legs to push off the pool bottom and/ or wall to assume a face float position. Then begin to flutter kick and add one crawl arm stroke cycle. Recover to a stand, taking a breath, and repeat.

Rhythmic Breathing

This technique is *the* correct way to continuously maintain a breathing pattern while doing the crawl stroke. Inhale and place your face in the water, exhaling immediately, expelling air in a steady stream. Without lifting your head out of the water to inhale, pivot your head to your right or left side (whichever is more comfortable). Remember, your mouth and nose just clear the water to take a bite of air. The clue to rhythmic breathing is in the underwater exhalation through both nose and mouth.

W.E.T. Drill
- *Breathe with Head Turn:* Stand in waist-deep water, with your head in center position. Inhale as your head turns to your breathing side toward your right *or* left shoulder. Exhale continuously as your head turns back to center. Repeat to same side, maintaining continuous pivoting motion. Then, bend forward from your waist, place your face in the water, and practice the sequence of rhythmic breathing, forming bubbles continuously as you exhale.

Rhythmic Breathing with Crawl Arm Stroke

The secret to comfort while swimming the crawl stroke is to get a steady supply of air. Rhythmic breathing is the coordinating of your arm strokes with your inhalation of air in a frequent, regular pattern. As you turn your head to your breathing side to inhale, the arm of the opposite side of your body is stretched out in front of you. Take a breath and pivot your head into the water, exhaling and forming bubbles as that arm passes down and straight under your body. Remember to exhale continuously, never hold your breath, and pivot your head to the same side for your next breath.

W.E.T. Drill
- *Stroke and Breathe:* Combine the crawl arm motion and rhythmic breathing while standing in place.

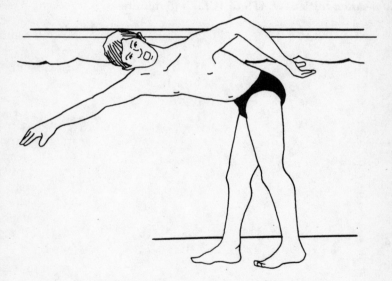

Rhythmic Breathing with Crawl Arm Stroke

DAY 2 WORKOUT

Distance: 2 laps (50 yards)
Total Time: 25 minutes

Warm-up with SWEATS to W.E.T.s (5 minutes)

Main Set (15 minutes)

W.E.T. Drills
Wall Stroke
Crawl Walk
Breathe with Head Turn
Stroke and Breathe

Distance: 2 laps
Lap 1   Float, glide, and flutter kick (with kickboard optional)
Lap 2   Combine crawl arm motion with flutter kick

Cool-down with SWEATS to W.E.T.s (5 minutes)

SWIM TIP: Experiment with breathing on both sides to determine your better breathing side. Then practice your rhythmic breathing on that side *only*.

LEVEL 1   **DAY 3**

SKILLS: Crawl Stroke—Arms, Legs and Rhythmic Breathing
Reading the Clock and Pulse Check

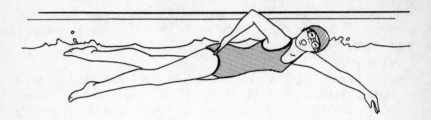

Crawl Stroke—Arms, Legs and Rhythmic Breathing

The combining of all parts of the crawl stroke allows you to swim continuously while breathing comfortably. To coordinate rhythmic breathing with every arm stroke cycle, take a breath by turning your head to your breathing side. Your arm on that side is at your thigh and is ready to recover. At the same time the opposite arm is extended forward for the catch, ready to pull. As you progress through the stroke, your face gradually enters the water, your extended arm comes down into the pull position, and your opposite arm recovers out of the water. Steadily increase the number of consecutive rhythmic breaths you can take each time you swim. Flutter kick steadily and continuously. Often your legs kick six times (called a six-beat kick) per arm stroke cycle.

W.E.T. Drill
- *Crawl Walk with Breathing:* Water walk forward in shallow water, combining crawl hand-over-hand arm motion and rhythmic breathing.

Reading the Clock and Pulse Check

The time has come to speak of clocks, time, and pulse checks.

A measure of your swim progress is the time it takes you to go a distance, whether it be one lap or a mile, or do a skill such as a glide, kick, or push-off.

You can measure your progress with pace clocks or wall clocks with sweep-second hands which are usually in the pool area. Or you can wear your own waterproof wristwatch or have someone time you. Learn how to keep one eye on the clock while you are working out.

The starting position on a pace clock is "0"; on a wall clock or wristwatch it is at 12 o'clock at the sixty-second marker; or on a digital watch set in a stopwatch mode.

As the clock hand reaches a starting position, begin practicing your skill. As soon as you finish, read the clock.

To measure the aerobic work you've done, check your pulse rate. See the section "Check Your Body" in chapter 1 to review how to take your pulse.

W.E.T. Drill
- *Wall Flutter Kick for Time—1 minute:* Begin flutter kicking either sitting on the edge, holding on to the wall, or with a kickboard. When the clock is at starting position, begin your flutter kicking drill for one minute. Continue kicking until the clock reads one minute or returns to its starting position. Take your pulse as you stop kicking.

DAY 3 WORKOUT

Distance: 3 laps (75 yards)
Total Time: 25 minutes

Warm-up with SWEATS to W.E.T.s (5 minutes)

Main Set (15 minutes)

W.E.T. Drills
   Flutter Kick on Wall
   Crawl Walk with Breathing
   Wall Flutter Kick—1 minute

Distance: 3 laps
   Lap 1   Crawl arm motion and flutter kick
   Lap 2   Crawl stroke, arms, legs and breathing
                    Rest
   Lap 3   Timed flutter kick or swim and pulse check
           Read the clock
           Record your time

Cool-down with SWEATS to W.E.T.s (5 minutes)

SWIM TIP: Record your time on your Timed Swims Progress Chart in Appendix D for your one-lap swim. Remember to check your pulse.

LEVEL 1 DAY 4

SKILL: Open Turn

Open Turn

Swimming laps without interruption is a key component of the training effect. A "turn" at the end of each lap makes continuous swimming possible by utilizing your momentum to start a new lap in a streamlined body position.

As you approach the wall, grasp the pool edge with your hand which has just recovered and is extended forward (see illustrations on page 48). Pull yourself toward the wall, bringing your knees into a tuck position in front of your body (# 1). Lower the shoulder of your free arm into the water and turn your body in the opposite direction, 180 degrees, swinging your legs and hips under you and bringing your feet flat against the pool wall (# 2). Take a breath with your head just above the water. Release your hand from the wall, swinging it over your shoulder near your forehead. Extend it just beneath the water's surface to join the other arm. Both arms are now stretched over your head.

Turn your toes downward to rotate your body to a face float position as indicated by the solid arrow on # 2. Then push off the wall with your legs with a streamlined body. As you glide in a streamlined body position, begin flutter kicking and add your arm stroke as you surface.

W.E.T. Drills
- *Sit-up:* Place your back against the corner of the pool, arms grasping the edge. Bend both knees, bringing them up to your chest. Twist your body and bring your legs toward the right. Extend your legs, bend them up, and return to center. Twist to the left, extend your legs, bend them up, and return to center. Repeat.
- *Tuck 'n' Turn:* Stand several feet from the wall. Push off from the bottom, glide and kick to the wall, arms stretched overhead. Grasp the pool edge with one hand, then tuck your knees to your chest. Turn 180°, adding the push-off from the wall. Practice the Tuck 'n' Turn, alternating the arm you lead with as you approach the wall to practice your open turn.

Open Turns

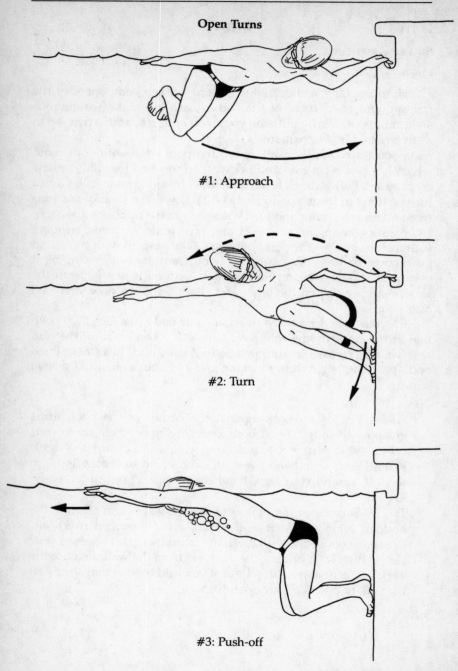

#1: Approach

#2: Turn

#3: Push-off

DAY 4 WORKOUT

Distance: 4 laps (100 yards)
Total Time: 25 minutes

Warm-up with SWEATS to W.E.T.s (5 minutes)

Main Set (15 minutes)

  W.E.T. Drills
    Sit-ups
    Tuck 'n' turn

  Distance: 4 laps

Lap 1	Crawl stroke: focus on good form
Laps 2–3	Crawl, with open turn—continuous swim
Lap 4	Crawl

Cool-down with SWEATS to W.E.T.s (5 minutes)

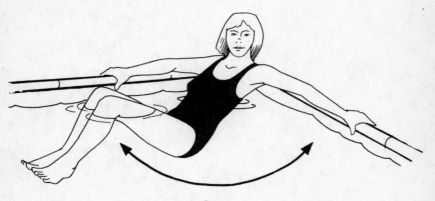

Sit-up

SWIM TIP: Lay the groundwork to swim farther, faster, and better through continuous swimming. Turns are the connecting links.

LEVEL 1   DAY 5

SKILL: Splashback Arm Stroke

Splashback Arm Stroke

The splashback arm stroke helps you complete the pulling motion of the crawl arm stroke to its fullest extent. With the splashback arm stroke you can overcome the common fault of shortening your stroke. It emphasizes the depth, direction, and follow-through of the pull. Your hand brushes past your thigh and forcefully splashes water back, breaking the surface as you begin your recovery.

W.E.T. Drills

- *Splashback drill:* Walk in chest-deep water with the crawl arm stroke and splash water backward behind you forcefully, as you finish the pull of each crawl arm stroke. You can also practice the splashback drill while holding a kickboard with one hand while splashing back with the other. Then reverse.
- *Push-ups:* Begin with your body facing the wall with hands on the pool's edge, shoulder-width apart. Straighten your elbows and lift your body out of the water. Hold for a moment and return to starting position.

DAY 5 WORKOUT

Distance: 5 laps (125 yards)
Total Time: (25 minutes)

Warm-up with SWEATS to W.E.T.s (5 minutes)

Main Set (15 minutes)

W.E.T. Drills
    Flutter kick with kickboard
    Splashback drill
    Push-ups

Distance: 5 laps

Laps 1–2	Crawl stroke and continuous swim
Lap 3	Splashback armstroke—crawl
Laps 4–5	Crawl continuous swim with splashback arm stroke

Cool-down with SWEATS to W.E.T.s (5 minutes)

SWIM TIP: Drills help you to learn skills correctly, and overcome faulty swim habits. For example, "splashback" gives you the exaggerated feeling of the crawl arm pulling motion. Once you're comfortable with the drill, incorporate it into your crawl arm motion without splashing.

LEVEL 1   DAY 6

SKILLS: High Elbow Recovery
Wide Hand Entry
Timed Swim and Pulse Check

High Elbow Recovery

During the recovery phase of your crawl arm stroke, exaggerate the lift of your elbow so that it is much higher than your hand. With your arm relaxed, trail your fingertips on the surface, just rippling the water. Keeping your elbow high, extend your arm forward in a 30- to 45-degree downward angle for your next catch.

W.E.T. Drill
- *Fingertip recovery:* Walk forward in chest-deep water with the crawl arm motion. As your arm recovers, bend and lift the elbow just high enough so that your fingertips skim the water's surface.

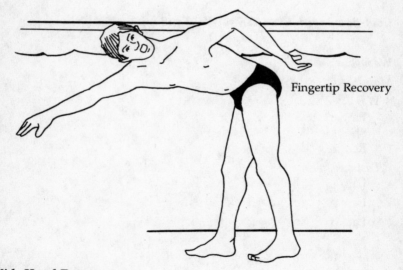

Fingertip Recovery

Wide Hand Entry

Another common fault among swimmers of the crawl stroke is pulling too narrow; that is, entry for the catch is too far inside the shoulder line or width. To correct this, the wide hand entry begins by entering or "catching" the hands just outside the shoulder line.

W.E.T. Drill
- *Shoulder-width kickboard pulls:* Hold kickboard sideways with hands on each end. Walk and stroke with one arm at a time,

shoulder width apart, past the outer edge of kickboard. If a kickboard is not available, exaggerate the shoulder-width entry of the catch.

Timed Swim and Pulse Check

You now have completed Level 1. Congratulations! By this time, it's a good idea to time yourself—if you haven't done so already—and measure your improvement. Use your waterproof watch, poolside wall, or pace clock to time one lap. As soon as you've completed your swim, check your time and pulse.

W.E.T. Drill
- *Reading the clock for a push-off* (see page 45): Wait until the second hand is at starting position. Then immediately push off, glide, recover, and read the clock.

DAY 6 WORKOUT

Distance: 6 laps (150 yards)
Total Time: 25 minutes

Warm-up with SWEATS to W.E.T.s (5 minutes)
Main Set (15 minutes)

W.E.T. Drills
Fingertip Recovery
Shoulder-Width Kickboard Pull
Reading the Clock with a Push-Off

Distance: 6 laps

Lap 1	Crawl stroke
Lap 2	Crawl stroke with high elbow recovery
Lap 3	Crawl stroke with wide hand entry
Laps 4–5	Crawl stroke—continuous swim
	Rest
Lap 6	Timed swim and pulse check
	Record your time and pulse in Appendix D

Cool-down with SWEATS to W.E.T.s (5 minutes)

SWIM TIP: Throughout your crawl arm stroke, your elbow is *always* higher than your hand. You're now on your way to improving your form.

Level 2

In Level 2 you'll learn the elementary and windmill backstroke. You'll also become more comfortable developing your treading skills. You will continue increasing your distance and crawl stroke efficiency. Your workout distance will increase from 3 laps (75 yards) to 12 laps (300 yards). Each workout in Level 2 will have a total time of 30 minutes. This includes a five-minute warm-up, a 20-minute main set of W.E.T. drills and laps and finishes with a five-minute cool-down. You also have an optional kick for two minutes. You can chart your progress on page 140. In Level 2 you will be learning the following skills in Days 7–12.

Day	Swim Skills
7	Back float and recovery
	Back glide with flutter kick
8	Treading
9	Back sculling
	Timed swim and pulse check—1 lap
10	Elementary backstroke arm motion
	Closed turn
11	Whip kick
	Elementary backstroke
12	Windmill backstroke
	Timed swim and pulse check—2 laps

LEVEL 2   DAY 7

SKILLS: Back Float and Recover
          Back Glide with Flutter Kick

Back Float and Recover

This important safety skill provides a smooth transition from your
back float to a standing position.

Assume a back float position by tilting your head back and leaning
your body backwards. Your feet leave the pool bottom and your chest,
hips, and legs rise toward the surface to a back float position. Keep
your arms at your sides underwater.

Recover to a stand by bending at the waist as if you were punched
in the abdomen: simultaneously draw your knees up to your chest,
lower your chin to your chest, and scoop your arms behind you in a
circular motion. This action is like that of seating yourself in a
chair.

If the back float is a new skill for you, it's advisable to concentrate
on the recovery phase first.

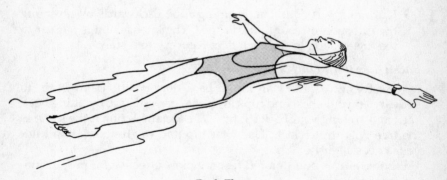

Back Float

W.E.T. Drills
- *Back float with kickboard support:* Place kickboard on abdomen for
  extra support while assuming back float position.
- *Back float at wall:* Position yourself with your back against the
  corner of the pool, and tilt your head back into the water. Grasp
  either wall, allowing hips and legs to rise to a back float. To
  recover, draw your knees to your chest, bring your head and
  shoulders forward and place your feet on pool bottom.

Back Float Recover

- *Back jump rope:* Simulate jumping rope backwards by reversing the direction of your "jump rope." The knee action is similar to the knee action in the back float recovery to a stand.

Back Glide with Flutter Kick

Walk backward and lean into a back float position and begin to glide. Keep your chest and hips high at water's surface by tilting head back and arching your back slightly. The kicking action is the same as the face float flutter kick. Use your hip and thigh muscles and flex your knees slightly.

Flexible ankles and pointed feet are most effective for propulsion.

W.E.T. Drill

- *Wall kick on back:* Place your back against the wall. Hold onto the pool edge, with arms extended to either side. Bring your legs up to the surface, adding the back flutter kick. Just barely break the surface, making water "boil." Kick for two minutes.

DAY 7 WORKOUT

Distance: 7 laps (175 yards)
Total Time: 30 minutes

Warm-up with SWEATS to W.E.T.s (5 minutes)

Main Set (20 minutes)

W.E.T. Drills
Backward jump rope
Back float at wall
Wall kick on back
Back float and recovery

Distance: 7 laps

Lap	1	Back float, glide and flutter kick
Laps	2–4	Crawl stroke
Lap	5	Back flutter kick
Laps	6–7	Crawl stroke

Cool-down with SWEATS to W.E.T.s (5 minutes)

SWIM TIP: For added safety, you can practice your back float and recovery with a partner supporting you from behind.

LEVEL 2   **DAY 8**

SKILL: Treading

Treading

Treading is a safety skill that enables you to stay afloat in deep water in a vertical position, with your head above water, and using as little energy as possible. To tread, your arms use a *sculling* motion and legs will kick in a bicycle *pedal action*. You can also use other leg kicks, e.g., scissor, eggbeater, frog, or whip kick.

Treading arm scull motion: You create the "Figure 8" sculling motion with your arms moving simultaneously away from the center of your body and back to the starting point as your palms press against the water in either direction. Stand in chest-deep water with your arms extended in front of you just below the water's surface. Begin with thumbs up, palms facing each other. Turn your thumbs down and press your hands out and away from each other until they are shoulder width apart; then turn your thumbs up and press your hands toward each other until your palms almost touch.

Sculling Arm Motion

Treading bicycle leg motion: Move your legs in a bicycle pedaling action as if you were sitting on a bicycle seat, your shoulders hunched over your knees.

W.E.T. Drills

- *Scull and hug:* Stand in chest-deep water. Extend your arms in front of you under the water with palms down. Sweep your arms outward and behind you, pressing water backward. Reverse sweep and press water forward with your palms, thumbs turned up. Your palms face and pass each other until your arms hug your body at shoulder level.

- *Marching leg steps:* Stand, then walk in shallow water, alternately bringing each knee up toward your chest as high as possible in a tuck position.
- *Total treading motion:* In chest-deep water, begin arm scull, bend the knees and add your bicycle leg motion, coordinating arms and legs simultaneously. Try not to let your feet touch the pool bottom. Gradually move to deeper water when you feel ready. If you are still a shallow-water swimmer, hold on to pool edge or ladder with one hand for added support when first learning to tread.

DAY 8 WORKOUT

Distance: 8 laps (200 yards)
Total Time: 30 minutes

Warm-up with SWEATS to W.E.T.s (5 minutes)

Main Set (20 minutes)

W.E.T. Drills
  Scull and hug
  Marching steps
  Total treading motion

Distance: 8 laps

Laps 1–2	Crawl stroke Tread for 30 seconds
Laps 3–4	Back flutter kick Tread for 30 seconds
Laps 5–6	Crawl stroke Tread for 30 seconds
Laps 7–8	Crawl stroke Tread for 30 seconds

Cool-down with SWEATS to W.E.T.s (5 minutes)

SWIM TIP: Treading is a safety skill as well as a great water exercise. Practice your treading between laps.

LEVEL 2   DAY 9

SKILLS: Back Sculling
         Timed Swim and Pulse Check

Back Sculling

From a back float position with arms extended out to the sides, add your flutter kick. Immediately begin to modify the wide arm treading scull by making smaller figure-eight movements as you scull your arms down to your sides from shoulder level to hip level. Bring your hands behind your hips, arching your palms so that the fingertips are pointing upward. Continue sculling underwater with smaller and faster figure-eight motions. Remember to inhale and exhale continuously.

W.E.T. Drills

- *Clap 'n' scull:* Walking backward in chest-deep water, move your hands in a figure-eight motion behind your back. When your hands are at their closest, "clap" or touch them together at the center of your back.
- *Foot support for scull:* From a back float position with heels on pool edge or ladder, add sculling arm motion to support your body in a stationary back float position.

Timed Swim and Pulse Check

See page 45.

DAY 9 WORKOUT

Distance: 9 laps (225 yards)
Total Time: 30 minutes

Warm-up with SWEATS to W.E.T.s (5 minutes)

Main Set (20 minutes)

W.E.T. Drills
Clap 'n' Scull
Foot Support for Scull

Distance: 9 laps

Laps 1–3	Crawl stroke
Lap 4	Back flutter kick with back sculling Tread
Laps 5–7	Crawl stroke
Lap 8	Back flutter kick with back sculling Rest
Lap 9	Timed swim and pulse check Record time and pulse check on page 137

Cool-down with SWEATS to W.E.T.s (5 minutes)

SWIM TIP: Sculling is basic to swimming better. It is a component of swim drills, strokes, as well as fundamental techniques for water safety, synchronized swimming, and water polo.

LEVEL 2   **DAY 10**

SKILLS: Elementary Backstroke Arm Motion
          Closed Turn for Crawl-Stroke

Elementary Backstroke Arm Motion

The elementary backstroke is a relaxing simultaneous stroke. The advantage of swimming on your back is that you can breathe freely since your face is out of the water. Your arms remain underwater throughout the stroke.

The *catch* takes place when your arms have reached the "V" position while you are floating on your back. *Pull* both arms straight down underwater to your thighs. Keep your hands at your sides and glide to take advantage of the momentum of the pull. *Recover* by drawing your arms up along the sides of your body, your hands reaching up under your armpit. Then extend your arms, reaching backwards underwater to the "V" or catch position.

Elementary Backstroke Arm Motion

Catch and Pull

Recovery

W.E.T. Drill
- *Stretch 'n' pull:* In a standing position, bring your arms from a "V" position just above shoulders straight down through the water to your sides. Draw your hands along your sides up to your armpits as if you were scratching an itch and quickly extend them back to the "V" position, ready for the "catch."

Closed Turn for Crawl Stroke

All turns have the same purpose: to use your body's momentum to turn 180 degrees and start your new lap in a streamlined body position. As your crawl stroke improves and you increase the number of laps you swim, you can replace the open turn with the more efficient closed turn.

Approach the wall with the crawl stroke as you would for the open turn, being sure you have just taken a good breath. Grasp the wall with your leading arm, tuck your knees and place your feet on the wall to turn. Remember to rotate your feet against the wall and push off into the streamlined glide position.

Transitional turns are those which you use to change direction from one stroke to another, e.g., backstroke to crawl.

W.E.T. Drill
- *Closed encounters:* Stand several strokes from the wall. Swim into the wall, practicing the closed turn, keeping your face underwater throughout the turn.

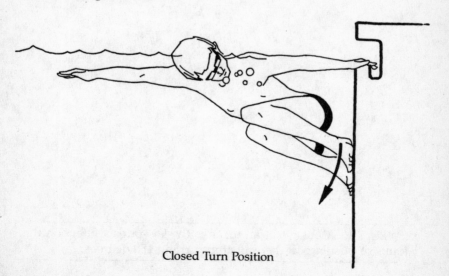

Closed Turn Position

DAY 10 WORKOUT

Distance: 10 laps (250 yards)
Total Time: 30 minutes

Warm-up with SWEATS to W.E.T.s (5 minutes)

Main Set (20 minutes)

W.E.T. Drills
 Stretch 'n' Pull
 Closed Encounters

Distance: 10 laps

Laps 1–2	Crawl stroke with closed turn
Lap 3	Elementary backstroke arm motion with flutter kick
Laps 4–7	Crawl stroke
Lap 8	Elementary backstroke arm motion with flutter kick
Laps 9–10	Crawl stroke with closed turn

Cool-down with SWEATS to W.E.T.s (5 minutes)

SWIM TIP: A benefit of all turns is the low-impact effect on the joints of pushing off the wall after turning 180 degrees.

LEVEL 2   **DAY 11**

SKILLS: Whip Kick
        Elementary Backstroke

Whip Kick

The leg motion for the elementary backstroke is a "whip" kick, a modification of the older, more conventional "frog" kick. Begin with a back float position, your feet close together near the water's surface and your toes pointed. With one movement, drop your heels and flex your feet toward the bottom. Next turn your feet outward as you extend your legs to a narrow "V" position, knees approximately hip-width apart. Then energetically bring your legs together so that your ankles meet. Your legs do not break the surface of the water during the entire whip kick. See illustrations on page 66.

W.E.T. Drill
- *Whip kick on pool edge:* Sit on pool edge with your legs extended straight out over the water, your toes pointed. Bend your knees, dropping your heels and just brushing the wall with them. Flex your feet and rotate them outward, separating them about hip width apart. Hold for the "glide."
- *Whip kick on the wall:* Place your back against the wall; grasp pool edge with your arms extended at either side, and assume a back float position. As you whip kick, keep your knees underwater by dropping your heels toward the pool bottom. If needed, use the corner of the pool for added arm support and comfort.

Elementary Backstroke

This full description of the elementary backstroke combines the arm motion and whip kick. Start in a back float position with your arms at your sides and your feet together. Your arms and legs move simultaneously. As you draw your arms up along the side of your body, bend your knees and lower your heels. When your arms extend into a "V" position, your heels will be extended approximately hip-width apart. Pull your arms straight down under the water to your sides while you snap your feet together. The sequence is "bend, extend, snap together, and glide." The glide is your moment of letting yourself rest while being propelled through the water from the momentum of your stroke. Inhale while you recover, as you are bending your arms and legs; exhale while you are pulling and snapping your feet together for the glide.

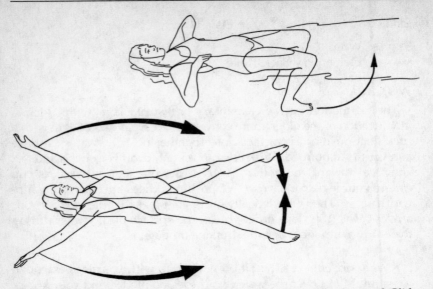

Elementary Backstroke Sequence: Bend, Extend, Snap Together, and Glide

W.E.T. Drill

- *Aqua Jumping Jacks:* Start in chest-deep water with legs together and arms at your sides. Jump up, extending arms to the side. As you come down, your legs separate into a "V" position, your arms on the water's surface. Jump again, bringing arms down and feet together.

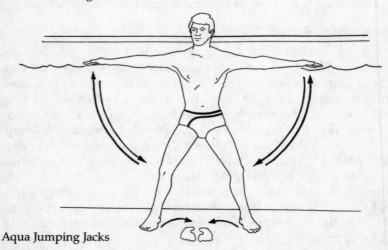

Aqua Jumping Jacks

DAY 11 WORKOUT

Distance: 11 laps (275 yards)
Total Time: 30 minutes

Warm-up with SWEATS to W.E.T.s (5 minutes)

Main Set (20 minutes)

W.E.T. Drills
   Whip kick on edge
   Whip kick on wall
   Aqua jumping jack

Distance: 11 laps

Lap	1	Whip kick floating on back with kickboard held against chest
Laps	2–4	Crawl stroke with closed turn
Lap	5	Elementary backstroke
Laps	6–7	Crawl stroke
Lap	8	Elementary backstroke
Laps	9–10	Crawl stroke—closed turn
Lap	11	Elementary backstroke

Cool-down with SWEATS to W.E.T.s (5 minutes)

SWIM TIP: Though the whip kick has superseded the "frog kick" for reasons of greater efficiency, many people find it to be an easier leg motion. In the frog kick, the knees bend outside hip width with feet close together and the legs extend into a wide "V" position before closing. Both the whip kick and the frog kick can be used for the elementary backstroke.

LEVEL 2   **DAY 12**

SKILLS: Windmill Backstroke
         Timed Swim and Pulse Check—2 laps

Windmill Backstroke

The other alternating stroke is the windmill backstroke. Basically it is the crawl stroke done on your back, with the arms working like the blades of a windmill. You breathe freely with your face out of the water.

Windmill arm motion: Start in a streamlined back float position with arms at your sides. Lift one arm straight overhead while continuing to keep the other at your side. With pinky finger leading, press the overhead extended arm downward into the water for the *catch* of the windmill backstroke arm motion. Sweep this arm straight down under the water for the *pull*. Brush past your thigh with your thumb to complete the pull. *Recover* by lifting your arm out of the water, leading with your pinky to continue straight back to the catch position.

While the first arm is in midair recovering, the other arm is pulling. Continue the alternating arm stroke motion with arms moving continuously and in opposition to each other.

Flutter leg motion and coordination: The backstroke flutter kick is similar to the crawl flutter kick. Your legs are close together and move in an alternating up and down motion. Your knees should stay loose

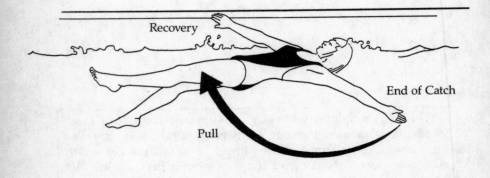

Windmill Backstroke

and flexible, making the water "boil" and just breaking the surface of the water. The coordination of arms, legs, and breathing is one breath and six kicks per arm cycle, an arm cycle being one right-arm pull and one left-arm pull. Inhale and exhale continuously so that you are completing a full breath every stroke cycle.

W.E.T. Drill
• *Alternating backward arm circles:* Alternately circle your arms backward, pulling under the water and recovering above the water. Make as large a backward circle as you can by raising your arm just past your ear and reaching as far back as you can.

DAY 12 WORKOUT

Distance: 12 laps (300 yards)
Total Time: 30 minutes

Warm-up with SWEATS to W.E.T.s (5 minutes)
Main Set (20 minutes)
  W.E.T. Drill
    Wall kick on back—2 minutes (see page 56)
    Alternating backward arm circles
  Distance: 12 laps

Lap	1	Windmill backstroke
Laps	2–3	Elementary backstroke
Lap	4	Windmill backstroke
Laps	5–7	Crawl stroke with one closed turn
Laps	8–10	Combination of strokes: 1 lap each of windmill backstroke, crawl, and elementary backstroke
		Rest
Laps	11–12	Timed swim and pulse check—2 laps Record your time on page 137

Cool-down with SWEATS to W.E.T.s (5 minutes)

SWIM TIP: The windmill backstroke helps to develop shoulder flexibility and increased range of motion. To help keep your body streamlined, keep your chest high.

Level 3

In Level 3 you'll learn the breaststroke. You will also be introduced to the S-shaped arm pull for the crawl stroke and windmill backstroke. The distance of your workouts will increase from 13 laps (325 yards) to 18 laps (450 yards) (approximately ¼ mile). Each workout in Level 3 will be 35 minutes. This includes a five-minute warm-up, a 25-minute main set of W.E.T. drills and laps and a five-minute cool-down. There is also an optional three-minute kick. Chart your progress on page 141.

In Level 3, you'll be learning the following skills in Days 13–18.

Day	Swim Skills
13	Breaststroke arm motion
14	Whip kick—face float position
	Breaststroke
15	"S"-shaped arm pull for crawl stroke
	Timed swim and pulse check—2 laps
16	Freestyle body roll
	Continuous swim—8 laps
17	Crossover kick
18	Windmill backstroke with bent arms pull
	Timed swim and pulse check—2 laps

LEVEL 3   **DAY 13**

SKILL: Breaststroke Arm Motion

Breaststroke Arm Motion

The breaststroke is a relaxing stroke in which the arms move simultaneously underwater.

In a streamlined face float body position, trace the outline of an upside-down heart shape. For the *catch*, begin with your arms extended forward, thumbs pointing down. Press your arms outward and downward, palms leading for the *pull*. Bend your elbows, keeping them up, and pull them back to shoulder level. Then bring your forearms together under your chest to complete the heart-shaped pattern. From this prayer-like position of hands and arms, *recover* underwater to the starting position by extending arms forward.

To breathe, your head lifts as you begin the arm stroke, and lowers with the recovery of your arm motion.

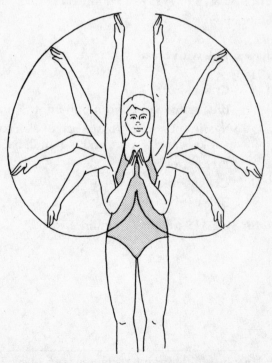

Breaststroke Heart-Shaped Arm Motion

W.E.T. Drills
- *Heart-shaped pull with breathing:* Standing, then walking in chest-deep water, practice the heart-shaped arm motion as you breathe. Begin with your face in the water and your arms extended in front of you, thumbs touching. Lift your head to inhale as you begin to pull arms outward. As hands move under your chest, place your face back in the water and exhale, extending your arms in front of you.
- *Breaststroke pull with pull-buoy:* Place pull-buoy between legs for support when practicing breaststroke pull.

DAY 13 WORKOUT

Distance: 13 laps (325 yards)
Total Time: 35 minutes

Warm-up with SWEATS to W.E.T.s (5 minutes)

Main Set (25 minutes)

W.E.T. Drills
Heart-shaped pull with breathing

Distance: 13 laps

Laps	1–3	Crawl stroke
Lap	4	Breaststroke pull (with pull-buoy, optional)
Laps	5–7	Medley of strokes, 1 lap each of elementary backstroke, crawl stroke, and windmill backstroke
Lap	8	Breaststroke pull
Laps	9–12	Crawl stroke
Lap	13	Breaststroke pull

Cool-down with SWEATS to W.E.T.s (5 minutes)

SWIM TIP: Your head lifts for inhalation as your upper arms and shoulders rise with the pull.

LEVEL 3 **DAY 14**

SKILLS: Whip Kick—Face Float Position
        Breaststroke

Whip Kick—Face Float Position

The breaststroke uses the same whip kick as the elementary backstroke. It can also be done with the frog kick—see illustration page 74. Review the whip kick in a back float position. Then turn over and take a face float position. Begin by bringing heels up toward buttocks and dropping your knees without breaking the water surface with your heels. Then flex your feet, and separate and extend your legs into a "V" position. Complete the kick by snapping legs together (as if squeezing water from a sponge). It is this quick, definite movement that provides the propulsion for the whip kick.

W.E.T. Drills

- *Karate kick:* Stand in waist-deep water with your right hand resting lightly on the pool edge. Bend your right knee and bring your right foot up behind you, close to your buttock. Then rotate your lower leg outward from the knee and touch the wall with your heel. Rotate your leg forward, finishing circle to resume the starting position. Repeat with the other leg.
- *Plié and jump (Plyometrics):* Begin in a plié (knees bent with feet flexed). As you straighten, jump up by using your leg muscles to explode off the bottom and point your toes. Return to starting position and repeat.

Breaststroke

Look at the Breaststroke Sequence illustrations on page 74. Begin in a streamlined body position with your arms and legs fully extended (# 1). As you begin your arm pull, lift your head for a breath as your shoulders rise naturally, and bend your knees to start your kick (#2). As your legs finish the kick, your arms recover to a glide position (#3) with body streamlined and face in the water exhaling (#4). Finish each lap with your hands reaching the wall simultaneously.

In the breaststroke, your arms and legs supply approximately equal propulsion.

W.E.T. Drill

- *Heart-shaped pull with knee bend:* Combine the heart-shaped pull with a knee bend in standing position. As you begin your pull, bend your knees. As you bring hands together for the recovery, straighten your legs.

Breaststroke Sequence

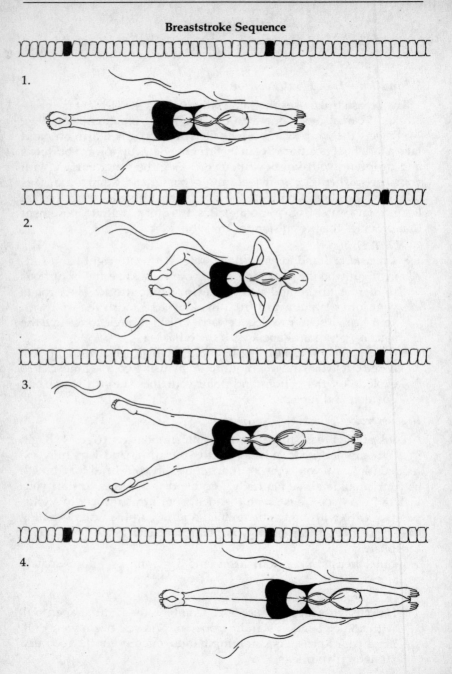

DAY 14 WORKOUT

Distance: 14 laps (350 yards)
Total Time: 35 minutes

Warm-up with SWEATS to W.E.T.s (5 minutes)

Main Set (25 minutes)

W.E.T. Drills
Karate kick
Plié and jump
Heart-shaped pull with knee bend

Distance: 14 laps

Lap	1	Breaststroke kick (whip or frog) with kickboard
Lap	2	Breaststroke
Laps	3–5	Crawl
Laps	9–11	Medley: breaststroke, crawl, windmill backstroke
Laps	12–14	Medley: breaststroke, crawl, windmill backstroke

Cool-down with SWEATS to W.E.T.s (5 minutes)

SWIM TIP: In breaststroke, recover your arms quickly for a streamlined glide.

LEVEL 3   **DAY 15**

SKILLS: "S"-shaped Arm Pull for Crawl Stroke
        Timed Swim and Pulse Check

"S"-shaped Arm Pull for Crawl Stroke

Techniques in all sports are not static. The challenge to athletes at all levels to attain greater speed and strength and to best harness their bodies' energy and momentum results in improved training methods and innovative techniques. For swimming, the development of the S-shaped arm pull in freestyle is an important example of this process.

In the crawl armstroke, you push water straight down and back from the *catch* like a paddle wheel. A more efficient arm motion to propel your body forward is called the "S-shaped pull." This *pull* or power phase is a difference between the crawl and freestyle (because the catch and recovery are essentially the same). This updated crawl stroke is incorporated into what is frequently called the freestyle.

"S"-Shaped Arm Pull

The "S"-shaped pull displaces "still" water rather than water that's already in motion. This enables you to move an increased volume of water with each stroke, which propels you forward with greater efficiency per stroke.

To perform the two-part S-shaped pull, trace a reverse letter S or question mark with your right hand by first pulling water outward and downward. As your hand passes your head, then pull inward, toward your waist (part 1). Next, press your hand back, moving it diagonally toward your thigh. Straighten and extend your arm as you accelerate the movement, as if you were throwing a ball in the direction of your feet (part 2). Repeat with the left arm, tracing a letter S or reverse question mark.

W.E.T. Drills
- *Single-arm "S" pull:* Standing in waist-deep water, place left hand on pool edge. Trace a reverse "S" pattern or question mark through the water with right arm. Change arms and trace an "S" pattern or reverse question mark with your left arm.
- *Catch-up "S" pull:* Begin with your arms extended, holding on to a kickboard turned widthwise for support. Walk in shallow water, tracing the "S"-pull pattern, one arm at a time. Wait or catch-up before starting stroke with other arm. This catch-up S-pull drill can also be done without a kickboard.

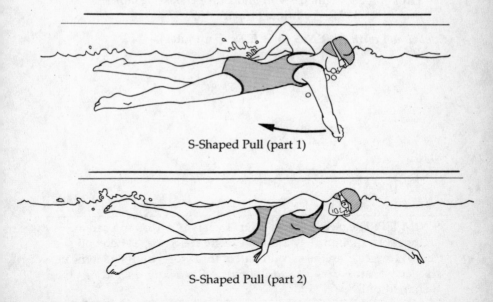

S-Shaped Pull (part 1)

S-Shaped Pull (part 2)

DAY 15 WORKOUT

Distance: 15 laps (375 yards)
Total Time: 35 minutes

Warm-up with SWEATS to W.E.T.s (5 minutes)

Main Set (25 minutes)

W.E.T. Drills
  Single-arm "S" pull
  Catch-up "S" pull

Distance: 15 laps

Laps	1–4	Crawl
Lap	5	Crawl arm stroke with "S" pull (with pull-buoy optional)
Laps	6–7	Crawl arm stroke
Lap	8	"S" pull (with pull-buoy optional)
Laps	9–11	Medley of strokes: elementary backstroke, breast-stroke, windmill backstroke
Laps	12–13	Crawl

Rest

Laps	14–15	Timed swim and pulse check—2 laps Record time on page 137

Cool-down with SWEATS to W.E.T.s (5 minutes)

SWIM TIP: The terms "crawl" and "freestyle" are often used inter-changeably, though they are not exactly the same. When you see "crawl/freestyle" in the second half of this program, it will indicate the crawl stroke with additional refinements including the S-shaped pull.

LEVEL 3   **DAY 16**

SKILLS: Freestyle Body Roll
             Continuous Swim—8 laps

Freestyle Body Roll

The S-shaped pull and the body roll together modify the traditional crawl stroke into the more efficient and powerful freestyle.

As you are *pulling* with your left arm, rotate your left shoulder down into the water approximately 45 degrees. The added leverage from your back and shoulder muscles during this roll creates momentum for your shoulder to roll and follow your hand into the water at the catch. When your right hand enters the water for the *catch*, the body roll reverses to the right side. This also allows a greater ease in turning your head for a breath.

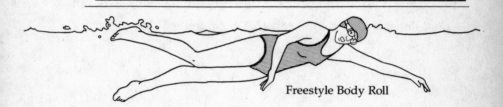

Freestyle Body Roll

W.E.T. Drills

• *Trunk Turn Variation:* Stand with your hands on your hips. Turn body and shoulders from side to side.
• *Stroke Punch:* In chest-deep water, alternately punch your arms forward underwater, allowing your shoulders to follow the full extension of your arm.

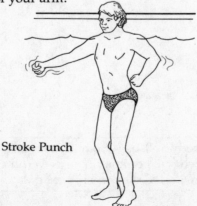

Stroke Punch

DAY 16 WORKOUT

Distance: 16 laps (400 yards)
Total Time: 35 minutes

Warm-up with SWEATS to W.E.T.s (5 minutes)

Main Set (25 minutes)

W.E.T. Drills
Trunk turn variation
Stroke punch

Distance: 16 laps

Laps 1–8	Crawl/freestyle continuous swim, rest if needed
Laps 9–10	Crawl/freestyle with S-pull and body roll
Laps 11–12	Backstroke and breaststroke
Laps 13–16	Alternate crawl/freestyle and windmill backstroke

Cool-down with SWEATS to W.E.T.s (5 minutes)

SWIM TIP: The body roll uses your strong back and shoulder muscles, so that each pull becomes more powerful and carries you a greater distance with the same energy expenditure.

LEVEL 3   **DAY 17**

SKILL: Crossover Kick

Crossover Kick

As each shoulder follows your arm into the water with the S-shaped pull, your hips naturally follow the roll of your shoulder. This results in your feet crossing at the lower part of the leg. To take advantage of this rotational momentum, the flutter kick is modified so that it becomes a balancing force for the freestyle. As the right shoulder rolls downward and the arm pulls, the right hip will also dip down, and the left foot will cross behind the right foot. For left-arm pull, the opposite occurs. See illustration for Crossover Fin Kick.

W.E.T. Drills
- *Sit 'n' Roll:* Sit on edge of the pool and alternately roll your hips from left to right. As your body rolls to the left, cross your right leg over the left. Alternate and roll to the right side.
- *Crossover Fin Kick:* Hold on to pool edge, while practicing crossover kick, wearing fins. Repeat using kickboard. Remember to turn your hips alternately from side to side.

Crossover Fin Kick

DAY 17 WORKOUT

Distance: 17 laps (425 yards)
Total Time: 35 minutes

Warm-up with SWEATS to W.E.T.s (5 minutes)

Main Set (25 minutes)

W.E.T. Drills
  Sit 'n' roll
  Crossover kick

Distance: 17 laps

Lap	1	Flutter kick (optional with fins and kickboard)
Lap	2	Crawl/freestyle (fins optional)
Laps	3–4	Crawl/freestyle (fins optional)
Laps	5–7	Crawl/freestyle (fins optional)
Lap	8	Crawl/freestyle with crossover kick
Laps	9–10	Crawl/freestyle with crossover kick
Laps	11–13	Crawl/freestyle with crossover kick
Laps	14–17	Medley of strokes: your choice

Cool-down with SWEATS to W.E.T.s (5 minutes)

SWIM TIP: Fins are like paddles that are extensions of the feet. They are available in different weights, shapes, and styles. They're great for developing flexibility, speed, higher body position, and for practicing the crossover kick.

LEVEL 3   **DAY 18**

SKILLS: Windmill Backstroke with Bent-Arm Pull
Timed Swim and Pulse Check

Windmill Backstroke with Bent-Arm Pull

We have seen how the S-shaped pull makes your crawl stroke more efficient. In the same way, your windmill backstroke is improved by adding the bent-arm pull.

As your arms move alternately, your body will roll naturally. Your left arm enters and *catches* under the water and then dips the body down to the right at a 45-degree angle. The arm then *pulls* downward and backward (#1). As you continue your pull, your elbow bends and moves toward your waist (#2). The accelerated or final part of the pull occurs when your hand reaches shoulder level. With your elbow close to your waist, your right forearm then rotates and presses "still" water straight down to your feet (as if you're throwing a ball down to your feet). Simultaneously, the left shoulder, with arm at your side, breaks the water's surface. It then *recovers* over head, with pinky up, and enters its catch, creating a body roll to the left side.

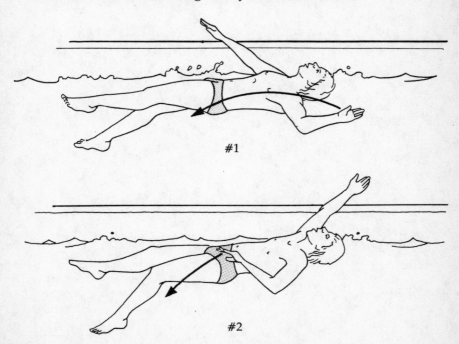

#1

#2

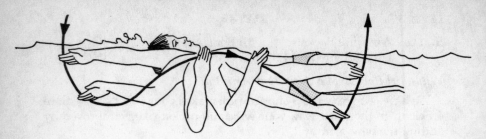

Full View of Bent-Arm Pull Motion

W.E.T. Drills
- *Trunk turn* (page 30)
- *Alternate ¼ turn jump:* Stand in chest-deep water with your elbows bent and your hands at water's surface. Jump and turn 90 degrees to the right by thrusting both hands to the left, full arm's length, thus moving the water in the direction opposite to your turn. Reverse direction.

DAY 18 WORKOUT

Distance: 18 laps (450 yards)
Total Time: 35 minutes

Warm-up with SWEATS to W.E.T.s (5 minutes)

Main Set (25 minutes)

W.E.T. Drills
  Trunk turn variation
  Alternate ¼ turn with jump

Distance: 18 laps

Lap	1	Flutter kick (with fins—optional)
Lap	2	Flutter kick—roll ¼ turn every 10 kicks
Laps	3–4	Windmill backstroke—flutter kick with fins
Laps	5–6	Bent-arm backstroke
Laps	7–14	Crawl/freestyle
Laps	15–16	Bent-arm backstroke
		Rest
Laps	17–18	Timed swim and pulse check—2 laps
		Record your time on Progress Chart, page 137

Cool-down with SWEATS to W.E.T.s (5 minutes)

SWIM TIP: In the bent-arm backstroke, the body roll originates in the shoulders and chest and travels down to the hips while the head remains still.

Level 4

In Level 4, you'll learn the sidestroke. You'll continue to refine your freestyle and add new training techniques to your workout. The distance of your workouts will continue to increase from 19 laps (475 yards) to 24 laps (600 yards) or approximately ⅓ mile. Each workout in Level 4 will be 40 minutes. This will include a five-minute warm-up, a 30-minute main set of W.E.T. drills and laps, and finish with a five-minute cool-down. You'll also have an optional four-minute kick in your main set. Chart your progress on page 142.

In Level 4 you'll learn the following skills:

Days	Swim Skills
19	Sidestroke arm motion
	Continuous swim—10 laps
20	Scissor kick
	Sidestroke
21	Kickboard skills
	Timed swim and pulse check—3 laps
22	Face-front sculling
	Easy-brisk pace
23	Stroke count
24	Quick lightning turns and push-offs
	Timed swim and pulse check—3 laps

LEVEL 4   **DAY 19**

SKILLS: Sidestroke Arm Motion
           Continuous Swim—10 laps

Sidestroke Arm Motion

The sidestroke is a relaxing stroke which is done with your head just above the surface of the water and your arms and legs remaining underwater. Begin in a streamlined glide position, lying on either side. Your right arm, also called your bottom arm because it's lower in the water, is extended overhead in line with your ear. Your left arm, also called your top arm, rests on your thigh. Your right arm *catches* in the extended position and *pulls*, with elbow bent, underneath your face, to your chest. At the same time the left arm recovers upward so that both arms are moving simultaneously toward each other, with your hands meeting at chest level. The left arm then *pushes* down toward your feet as your right arm *recovers*, extending overhead. A glide phase follows and the stroke cycle begins again. See illustration on page 88. If you were to change sides, the left arm would be called your bottom arm while the right arm becomes the top arm. To change the side on which you're swimming, tuck your knees to your chest and extend your legs to the side in the opposite direction.

W.E.T. Drills
- *Sidestroke Float Position:* The sidestroke float position prepares you for the sidestroke itself. Hold a kickboard lengthwise comfortably under each arm. Extend one arm (the "bottom arm") in a side-glide position with your ear resting on your arm. Your other arm holding another kickboard lengthwise (the "top arm") is resting along the side of your body on your hip, your legs together and extended. You are now balanced in a sidestroke float position.
- *Apple Picking:* This drill simulates the sidestroke arm motion. Begin by standing in chest-deep water. Extend one arm overhead, reach and "pick an apple from a tree." Place it in the other hand at chest level; then that hand throws it downward (as if into a basket). Reach for another "apple." Then bring your hands underwater, arms extended sideways. Practice "apple picking" underwater.
- *Accordion Squeeze:* Simulate playing the accordion, expanding it to its full width and contracting it, hands meeting at chest level.

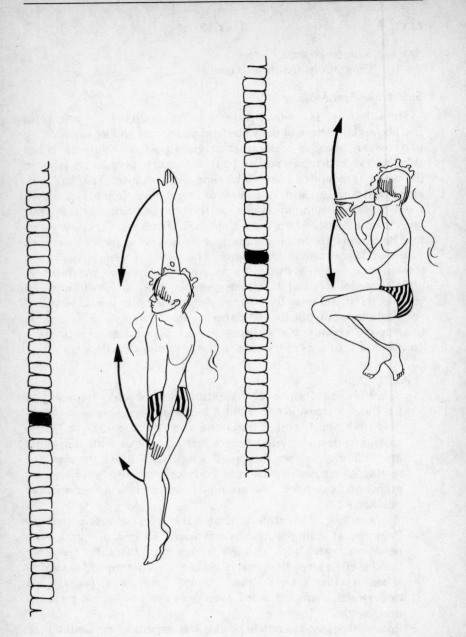

DAY 19 WORKOUT

Distance: 19 laps (475 yards)
Total Time: 40 minutes

Warm-up with SWEATS to W.E.T.s (5 minutes)

Main Set (30 minutes)

W.E.T. Drills
Sidestroke float position
Apple picking
Accordion squeeze

Distance: 19 laps

Laps	1–2	Breaststroke
Laps	3–4	Elementary backstroke
Laps	5–6	Breaststroke
Lap	7	Back flutter kick
Laps	8–9	Windmill backstroke Rest
Laps	10–19	Crawl/freestyle; 10-lap continuous swim

Cool-down with SWEATS to W.E.T.s (5 minutes)

SWIM TIP: Challenge your swimming endurance by completing a 10-lap continuous swim.

LEVEL 4   **DAY 20**

SKILLS: Scissor Kick
　　　　　Sidestroke

Scissor Kick

In the sidestroke kick, your legs separate and come together similar to the blades of a pair of scissors.

Begin in an extended glide position, with your legs together. Tuck your knees toward your chest. Then extend your legs in a stride or scissor position with top foot flexed and forward, and bottom leg back with toes pointed. Sharply snap your legs together for propulsion and finish in the glide position, legs together.

W.E.T. Drill

• *Scissors Lunge:* Stand in chest-deep water with your feet together. Take a long lunge sideward with one leg bent at the knee, while your back leg remains straight. Draw your back leg up to meet the front leg as it straightens. Continue lunging forward; then change directions.

Sidestroke

Sidestroke is a two-part stroke, beginning in a streamlined glide position on either side. In part 1 both arms and legs move from a glide position to the midpoint of the body as you inhale. Part 2 is where both arms and legs meet in a tuck position and then extend and return to a streamlined glide position as you exhale.

W.E.T. Drill

• *Sidestroke Walk:* Combine Scissors Lunge with Accordion Squeeze. Stand with your legs together and your arms held out to the sides at shoulder level, your palms facing forward. Take a step sideward with one foot, bending your knees as you bring your arms together to meet underwater at your chest with your elbows bent (part 1). Then stretch your arms out to the side and bring your legs together and straighten (part 2). Repeat, stepping in the same direction. Then reverse direction.

Sidestroke Sequence

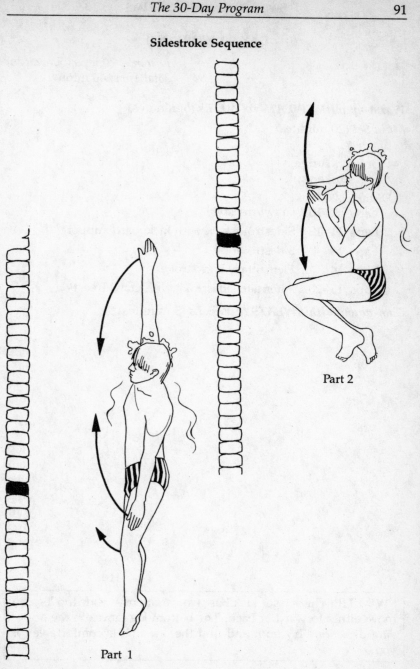

Part 1

Part 2

DAY 20 WORKOUT

Distance: 20 laps (500 yards)
Total Time: 40 minutes

Warm-up with SWEATS to W.E.T.s (5 minutes)

Main Set (20 minutes)

W.E.T. Drills
Scissors lunge
Sidestroke walk

Distance: 20 laps

Laps	1–10	Crawl/freestyle
Laps	11–12	Sidestroke kick with kickboard support
Lap	13	Sidestroke
Lap	14	Elementary backstroke
Laps	15–20	Alternate sidestroke with crawl/freestyle

Cool-down with SWEATS to W.E.T.s (5 minutes)

SWIM TIP: The scissor kick has two variations—your top leg can move either forward or back. The bottom leg moves in the opposing direction. Try both and find the one that is comfortable for you.

LEVEL 4   **DAY 21**

SKILLS: Kickboard Skills
         Timed Swim and Pulse Check

Kickboard Skills

The kickboard can be used for more than practicing your kicking. It can also be used as a resistance device for improving your body position and skills.

W.E.T. Drills
- *Kickboard Press:* Hold the kickboard widthwise with your hands on either side of the board. Use your upper arm (triceps) strength to press the board underwater, straightening your elbows. Then lift the board past the starting position to an overhead position to create a waterfall effect.
- *Overhead Kickboard Twist:* Hold the kickboard widthwise, with your arms extended overhead. Twist the board alternately to right and left, simulating the body roll.

Sample Kickboard Skills

The kickboard can also be used for coordinating stroke components.

Hold the kickboard lengthwise with your hands at the bottom of the board. This allows space for your face to be in the water when you are in the streamlined body position. Put your face into the water and begin your flutter kick with or without fins. Turn your head to your breathing side to inhale; turn your face into the water to exhale underwater. Then practice on your nonbreathing side.

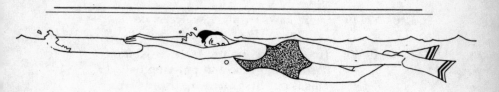

W.E.T. Drill
- *Kick and Breathe—on both sides:* In front float position, hold on to the pool edge with your hand in "bracket" position against the wall. The hand on your nonbreathing side grasps the pool edge. The hand on your breathing side is pressed against the pool wall, about one foot underwater with fingers pointing downward. Begin your flutter kicking; then add rhythmic breathing. Reverse your arms and practice rhythmic breathing on your nonbreathing side.

DAY 21 WORKOUT

Distance: 21 laps (525 yards)
Total Time: 40 minutes

Warm-up with SWEATS to W.E.T.s (5 minutes)

Main Set (30 minutes)

W.E.T. Drills
Kickboard press
Overhead kickboard twist
Kick and breathe—on both sides

Distance: 21 laps

Laps 1–2	Flutter kick and rhythmic breathing with kickboard support
Laps 3–4	Crawl/freestyle pull
Laps 5–10	Crawl/freestyle
Laps 11–16	Medley of strokes: alternate between backstroke and sidestroke
Laps 17–19	Swim kick–swim; crawl/freestyle
	Rest
Laps 19–21	Timed swim and pulse check—3 laps
	Record your time and pulse on page 137
	This is our first three-lap timed swim

Cool-down with SWEATS to W.E.T.s (5 minutes)

SWIM TIP: Experiment with kickboard. Create your own W.E.T. drills. Use the kickboard to help strengthen upper body.

LEVEL 4   **DAY 22**

SKILLS: Face Front Sculling
             Easy/Brisk Pace

Face Front Sculling

Sculling is a very important skill that helps to improve your stroke efficiency. It is especially helpful in perfecting the "catch" of each armstroke. Sculling provides continuous support and propulsion.

In a face float position, extend your arms forward, shoulder-width apart. With fingers pointed downward, create a "figure-eight" motion which moves your body head first. You can use hand paddles as shown in the illustration. For added support, flutter kick or place a pull-buoy between your legs at your upper thighs.

Sculling with Hand Paddles

W.E.T. Drill
- *Front Scull and Walk:* Walk forward in chest-deep water with your hands extended in front of you underwater, shoulder-width apart. With fingers pointed downward, describe a continuous "figure-eight" motion with your hands.

Easy/Brisk Pace

This variation of swim speeds is a technique created by Swedish athletes to increase aerobic capacity. It is known as "fartlek" training (sorry, it's not a dirty word!). After you swim a lap at a fast or brisk pace, swim the next lap at a slow or easy pace. This requires you to work at an overload, training your body to use oxygen more efficiently.

W.E.T. Drill
- *Walk/run:* Alternate running and walking in chest-deep water for one minute each. Repeat twice without stopping.

DAY 22 WORKOUT

Distance: 22 laps (550 yards)
Total Time: 40 minutes

Warm-up with SWEATS to W.E.T.s (5 minutes)
Main Set (30 minutes)

W.E.T. Drill
Front scull and walk
Walk/run

Distance: 22 laps

Laps	1–4	Easy crawl/freestyle
Lap	5	Face front scull (pull-buoy optional)
Laps	6–10	Easy/brisk pull—crawl/freestyle—alternate each lap
Lap	11	Scull
Laps	12–16	Easy/brisk swim—crawl/freestyle—alternate each lap
Lap	17	Scull
Laps	18–21	Easy/brisk kick—crawl/freestyle—alternate each lap
Lap	22	Scull

Cool-down with SWEATS to W.E.T.s (5 minutes)

SWIM TIP: Because sculling is a slow movement, it gives you the time to get the "feel of the water." It is especially important for the "catch" of all strokes.

LEVEL 4   **DAY 23**

SKILL: Stroke Count

Stroke Count

Doing a stroke count periodically is a way to see improvement in your stroke efficiency and power. Count the number of strokes you take (considering each hand entry as one stroke) to complete one pool length. Then try to lower the number of strokes you use for the next length.

W.E.T. Drill
- *Standing stroke count:* Standing in place, count the number of arm strokes you take for one minute. Rest one minute. Then repeat and lower your standing stroke count, pulling with more power but maintaining the same pace of arm recovery.

DAY 23 WORKOUT

Distance: 23 laps (575 yards)
Total Time: 40 minutes

Warm-up with SWEATS to W.E.T.s (5 minutes)

Main Set

W.E.T. Drill
Standing stroke count

Distance: 23 laps

Laps	1–6	Crawl/freestyle
Laps	7–12	Crawl/freestyle, alternate laps of kicking, pulling, swimming (one lap each)
Lap	13	Stroke count, crawl/freestyle
Lap	14	Stroke count (try to lower your stroke count by one)
Laps	15–18	Medley of strokes—your choice
Laps	19–23	Stroke count, crawl/freestyle

Cool-down with SWEATS to W.E.T.s (5 minutes)

SWIM TIP: D.P.S., or Distance Per Stroke, is another way of measuring your stroke efficiency. Measure the distance you propel yourself forward with each stroke. Increase that distance by moving more water backward and with greater force. Stroke counts can be used for all strokes.

LEVEL 4   **DAY 24**

SKILLS: Quick Lightning Turns and Push-offs
         Timed Swim and Pulse Check

Quick Lightning Turns and Push-offs

Although each stroke has a slightly different approach to the wall at the end of a lap, the turns are similar in that they use your swim speed to turn 180 degrees as quickly as possible.

When swimming the alternating strokes and the sidestroke variation, touch the wall with your leading arm. The body then tucks, turns 180 degrees and pushes off the wall. With the simultaneous strokes, you touch with both hands, then drop one arm, and then extend it in the opposite direction. Then, complete your 180-degree turn, finishing with your push-off into a streamlined body position.

W.E.T. Drill
- *Quick Lightning Turn:* Stand with one hand touching edge, arm extended, while other arm is extended in the direction of your push-off. Tuck knees up and place feet on wall. With your body in side position, duck your head just underwater as your wall arm bends and quickly brushes past your forehead in a salute position. Your hands then meet overhead and legs straighten for push-off. Repeat with opposite arm leading. Then begin with both hands touching wall simultaneously as in breaststroke and butterfly stroke you'll learn next. Extend one arm in direction of push-off and continue your quick lightning turn.

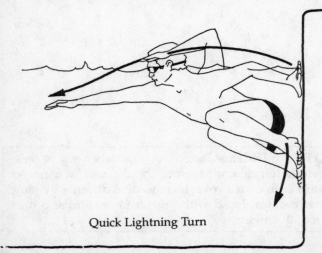

Quick Lightning Turn

DAY 24 WORKOUT

Distance: 24 laps (600 yards)
Total Time: 40 minutes

Warm-up with SWEATS to W.E.T.s (5 minutes)

Main Set (30 minutes)

W.E.T. Drill
Sit-up (page 47)
Quick lightning turn

Distance: 24 laps

Laps 1–8	Crawl/freestyle with quick lightning turns
Laps 9–14	Crawl/freestyle, alternate laps of kicking, pulling, swimming (2 laps each)
Laps 15–18	Medley of strokes—your choice
Lap 19	Windmill backstroke, stroke count
Lap 20	Windmill backstroke, stroke count—lower by one
Lap 21	Crawl/freestyle easy Rest
Laps 22–24	Timed swim and pulse check—3 laps Record your time on page 137

Cool-down with SWEATS to W.E.T.s (5 minutes)

SWIM TIP: Your turns can affect your time for your three-lap timed swim. The wall won't move, so anticipate where it is. Touch the wall and make a quick lightning turn, rather than "hanging out" at the wall!

Level 5

In Level 5, you'll learn the exciting butterfly. Give it the good old college try! If, however, you have any back problems, you may want to substitute another stroke for the butterfly. You'll also continue to add to training techniques and official Individual Medley (butterfly, backstroke, breaststroke, and freestyle). The distance will increase from 25 laps (625 yards) to 30 laps (750 yards). Each workout in Level 5 will take approximately 45 minutes. This will include a five-minute warm-up, a 35-minute main set, and finish with a five-minute cooldown. There is also an optional five-minute kick. Your 30th lap concludes this program. You can review this program from Day 1, but by all means continue to swim toward "The Magic Mile." As before, chart your progress on page 143.

Day	Swim Skill
25	Butterfly arm motion
	Timed rest intervals
26	Dolphin kick
	Butterfly stroke with single-beat kick
27	Alternate breathing for crawl/freestyle
	Butterfly, double-beat kick
	Timed swim and pulse check—3 laps
28	Flip turn
	Speed variations
29	Sculling with hand paddles
	Official Individual Medley
30	Even-paced swimming
	Timed swims and pulse check (1, 2, 3 laps)

LEVEL 5   **DAY 25**

SKILLS: Butterfly Arm Motion
        Timed Rest Intervals

Butterfly Arm Motion

The butterfly, a simultaneous stroke, is the most energetic and challenging stroke. The armstroke is similar to the S-shaped pull in freestyle. However, because the arms move at the same time tracing a "keyhole," there is no body roll.

For the *catch*, extend your arms underwater, shoulder-width apart, thumbs downward. *Pull* your arms outward and downward, beginning the "keyhole arm pattern." Then bring your hands together under your abdomen, near your waist, elbows bent about 90 degrees, and press the water backward toward your feet. When your arms are almost fully extended, with your hands near your hips, the *recovery* begins. Your arms recover out of the water, with elbows leading as they swing forward to the catch or starting position.

Take your breath at the end of the arm pull, just as your arms are beginning to recover. Lift your chin forward just enough to take a breath. Then lower your head immediately to exhale and recover your arms back to the catch position.

W.E.T. Drills

- *Double arm circles:* Stand, then walk, practicing double arm circles with S-pull pattern. Brush your thumbs past your thighs before recovering arms out of water. This is similar to the jump-rope (page 38) arm motion.
- *Butterfly lunge:* Stand with your back against the pool wall, your arms extended to the sides, holding the edge. Place your feet on the wall, arching your back slightly. As you push off from the wall with your legs, lunge forward by recovering your arms over the water with the butterfly arm pull.

Timed Rest Intervals

Training with timed rest intervals consists of laps which are interrupted by short specified rest periods. This puts into action the training effect principle of overload.

W.E.T. Drill

- *Take "30":* Begin double arm circles for 30 seconds. Then rest for 30 seconds. Repeat.

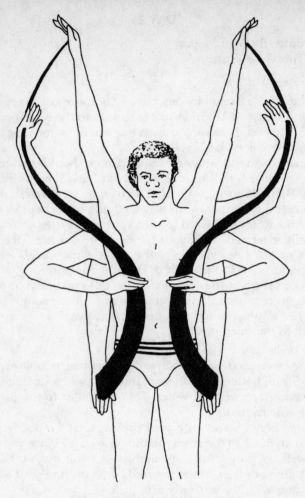

Butterfly "Keyhole" Armstroke

DAY 25 WORKOUT

Distance: 25 laps (625 yards)
Total Time: 45 minutes

Warm-up with SWEATS to W.E.T.s (5 minutes)

Main Set (35 minutes)

W.E.T. Drills
   Double arm circles
   Butterfly lunge
   Take 30—double arm circles

Distance: 25 laps

Laps	1–2	Crawl/freestyle; rest 30 seconds
Laps	3–4	Breaststroke; rest 30 seconds
Laps	5–8	Medley of strokes—your choice; rest 1 minute
Laps	9–16	Crawl/freestyle; rest 1 minute
Laps	17–20	Medley of strokes—your choice; rest 2 minutes
Laps	21–22	Crawl/freestyle; rest 1 minute
Laps	23–24	Sidestroke; rest 1 minute
Lap	25	Easy crawl/freestyle

Cool-down with SWEATS to W.E.T.s (5 minutes)

SWIM TIP: The "keyhole" butterfly arm stroke is similar to the freestyle "S" pull, with your arms moving simultaneously but without a body roll. The right arm traces a reverse "S" pattern or question mark while the left arm traces an "S" pattern or reverse question mark.

Rx REMINDER: If you have any back concern, substitute other strokes for the butterfly in your workouts.

LEVEL 5   **DAY 26**

SKILLS: Dolphin Kick
         Butterfly Stroke with Single Beat Kick

Dolphin Kick

The dolphin kick is used for the butterfly stroke. Your legs move up and down, similar to the flutter kick but in unison. A wave-like body motion is created by bringing your hips up, with buttocks breaking the surface of the water as your legs kick on the downbeat. On the upbeat, your feet should barely break the surface.

W.E.T. Drills

- *Sit 'n' kick:* Sit on the pool edge, with your knees bent. Drop your heels to touch wall, then simultaneously straighten your knees and lift your legs to water's surface, toes pointed. (You can use fins for added propulsion as shown here.)

Sit 'n' Kick

- *Body wave:* In deep water, hold on to the pool edge with one arm for support, keeping your body in a vertical position. With your legs together, press your hips alternately forward and backward, keeping your knees relaxed and allowing your hips and legs to move in a dolphin-like movement. Add fins to get the accentuated feeling of the body wave.

Butterfly Stroke with Single-Beat Kick

Although butterfly is normally done with a two-beat kick per arm stroke, the coordination of your arm and leg motion is best learned by starting with a single-beat kick per arm stroke. Begin in an extended face float position, arms extended underwater, shoulder-width apart for the *catch* (#1). Bend your legs as you bend your arms for the pull (#2) and straighten your legs as you bring your arms above the water for the recovery (#3). Lift your head for a breath as your shoulders rise during your pull.

W.E.T. Drill

- *Rope jump variation:* Simulate jumping rope without actually "jumping" or clearing the rope. Stand with your arms forward on the water's surface. As your arms circle downward into the water, bend your knees. As your arms brush by your thighs and recover out of the water, straighten your legs. This simulates the coordinating of the butterfly arms and legs with a single-beat kick.

Butterfly Stroke with Single Beat Kick

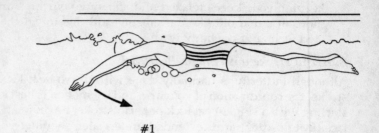

#1

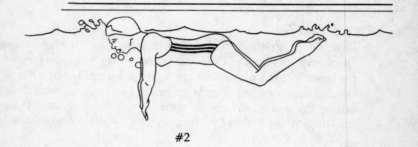

#2

#3

DAY 26 WORKOUT

Distance: 26 laps (650 yards)
Total Time: 45 minutes

Warm-up with SWEATS to W.E.T.s (5 minutes)
Main Set (35 minutes)

W.E.T. Drills
  Sit 'n' kick
  Body wave
  Rope jump variation

Distance: 26 laps

Laps	1–4	Crawl/freestyle
Lap	5	Dolphin kick (kickboard optional)
Laps	6–9	Crawl/freestyle
Lap	10	Dolphin kick (kickboard optional)
Lap	11	2 strokes butterfly; finish with stroke of your choice
Lap	12	3 strokes butterfly; finish with stroke of your choice
Lap	13	4 strokes butterfly; finish with stroke of your choice
Lap	14	5 strokes butterfly; finish with stroke of your choice (use of fins optional for all of the above)
Laps	15–18	Crawl/freestyle
Laps	19–20	Dolphin kick
Laps	21–26	Medley of strokes—your choice

Cool-down with SWEATS to W.E.T.s (5 minutes)

SWIM TIP: To get the wave-like dolphin movement you can experiment using fins. You can also use fins to develop more propulsion, power, and flexibility. You're not cheating!

Level 5　　　　　　　**DAY 27**

Skills: Alternate Breathing for Crawl/Freestyle
　　　　　Butterfly Stroke—Double Beat Kick
　　　　　Timed Swim and Pulse Check—3 laps

Alternate Breathing for Crawl/Freestyle

Alternate or bilateral breathing is the turning of the head to inhale every *third* arm stroke with your crawl/freestyle instead of every second arm stroke. This breathing pattern means you turn your head to both the right and left sides of your body to inhale. It is an effective way to balance your stroke, because the arm on your nonbreathing side tends to pull harder when you exhale. Your shoulder and back muscles on both sides of your body are strengthened equally with alternate breathing. And the added advantage is that it increases the training effect.

You can think of alternate breathing as "orthopedics" for your stroke.

W.E.T. Drills
- *Rhythmic breathing*: Practice rhythmic breathing with crawl arm motion on your nonbreathing side.
- *Three strokes 'n' breathe:* Stand, then walk and take three crawl arm stroke motions while you're exhaling into the water before inhaling on your breathing side. Continue, taking three arm stroke motions, so that your next inhalation is on your nonbreathing or opposite side. Repeat.

Butterfly Stroke—Double Beat Kick

Ideally in butterfly, there are two dolphin kicks per arm stroke. To coordinate arms and legs with a double beat kick, start in a glide position with your arms ready to catch. Kick for first downbeat, then stroke with your arms, bringing your legs to move for the upbeat. Begin the kick for the second downbeat when your hands are finishing the pull and your head lifts forward to breathe. Your arms recover out of the water as your feet move for the upbeat. Begin the first kick again just after your hands enter the catch position to begin a new stroke cycle.

W.E.T. Drills
- *Rope jump variation* Add a second knee bend just as arms recover.
- *One-arm butterfly:* Stand and pull with one arm at a time as knees bend and straighten twice (double beat kick). Repeat with other arm.

DAY 27 WORKOUT

Distance: 27 laps (675 yards)
Total Time: 45 minutes

Warm-up with SWEATS to W.E.T.s (5 minutes)

Main Set (35 minutes)

W.E.T. Drills
Rhythmic breathing on nonbreathing side
Kick and breathe on another side
Three strokes 'n' breathe
Jump rope double jump
One-arm butterfly

Distance: 27 laps

Laps 1–4	Crawl/freestyle Odd-numbered lengths, regular breathing side Even-numbered lengths, nonbreathing side
Lap 5	Right-arm pull with dolphin kick (kickboard optional)
Lap 6	Left-arm pull with dolphin kick (kickboard optional)
Lap 7	Butterfly
Lap 8	Dolphin kick with kickboard
Laps 9–16	Crawl/freestyle—alternate breathing on every other lap
Laps 17–20	Medley of strokes, stroke choice
Laps 21–24	Alternate butterfly and backstroke Rest
Laps 25–27	Timed swim and pulse check—3 laps Record time on page 137

Cool-down with SWEATS to W.E.T.s (5 minutes)

SWIM TIP: Alternate breathing is especially valuable for open-water swimming so you can locate the shoreline, avoid obstructions, and keep an eye on your fellow swimmer.

LEVEL 5   **DAY 28**

SKILLS: Flip Turn
         Speed Variations

Flip Turn

The flip turn is used with the crawl/freestyle stroke, and properly done is the ultimate in turning economy.

Approach the wall. Tuck your chin to your chest. Your extended arm pulls downward as legs dolphin kick to initiate the tuck. The arms circle backward, pressing water toward your face, which helps to lift your hips over your head. Rotate your body to the side as your feet touch the wall. Then push off into a streamlined body position.

W.E.T. Drills

- *Front tuck somersault:* Practice this in deep water, starting in a face float position with your hands at your sides. Drop your chin to your chest, tuck your knees to your chest, and push water backward with a scooping arm circle motion, beginning at your hips going toward your head, as if you're splashing water in your face. This movement flips your body over in a somersault.
- *Swim 'n' Tuck*: Begin five yards from the wall. As you approach the wall, do a front tuck somersault.
- *Flip Turn*: Swim and tuck. As your hips flip over your head, come out of the tuck and touch your feet to the wall. Rotate to a face front position and push off into a streamlined glide.

Flip Turn Sequence

Approach

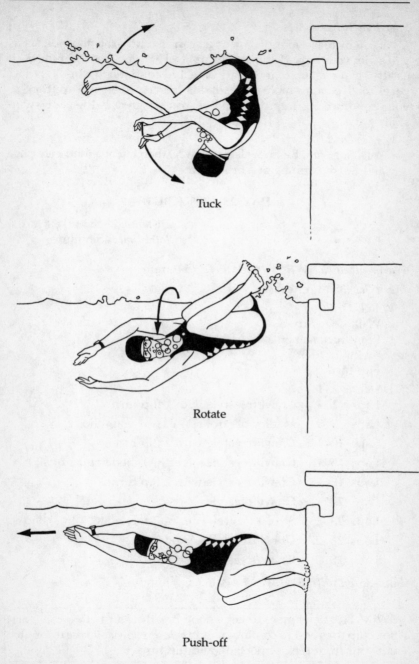

Tuck

Rotate

Push-off

Speed Variations

As you increase your distance you can also vary the pace you set as you swim your laps. Begin slowly and feel like you're swimming very easily. Then pick up to moderate pace and continue to a brisk, or fast pace. You'll become more aware of this "perceived energy exertion" as your conditioning improves and as you progress with your swim skills.

W.E.T. Drill
- *Walk, jog, run:* Begin walking slowly; then jog at a moderate pace and finish running at a brisk pace.

DAY 28 WORKOUT

Distance: 28 laps (700 yards)
Total time: 45 minutes

Warm-up with SWEATS to W.E.T.s (5 minutes)

Main Set (35 minutes)

W.E.T. Drills
Walk, jog, run
Front tuck somersault
Swim 'n' tuck
Flip turn

Distance: 28 laps

Laps	1–4	Crawl/freestyle with 1 flip turn
Laps	5–9	Medley of strokes—easy—your choice
Laps	10–14	Crawl/freestyle with 2 flip turns
Laps	15–17	Crawl/freestyle—1 easy, 1 moderate, 1 brisk lap
Laps	18–21	Crawl/freestyle with 2 flip turns
Lap	22	Crawl/freestyle—brisk
Laps	23–25	Stroke choice—1 easy, 1 moderate, 1 brisk lap
Laps	26–27	Crawl/freestyle—moderate
Lap	28	Crawl/freestyle—brisk

Cool-down with SWEATS to W.E.T.s (5 minutes)

SWIM TIP: Remember to get a good breath of air before you start your flip turn and to continuously *exhale through your nose* throughout your front tuck somersault and flip turn.

LEVEL 5   **DAY 29**

SKILLS: Sculling with Hand Paddles
          Official Individual Medley

Sculling with Hand Paddles

Hand paddles are like fins for your hands. They are used as training accessories because they require additional energy to overcome the resistance of the water, but give you additional propulsion. They should be used carefully. Listen to your body to avoid soreness of arm and shoulder muscles.

Hand paddles can be used for all strokes. To get the feel of the propulsion of hand paddles, try the sculling motion in a vertical or standing position.

W.E.T. Drill

- *Vertical scull:* Wearing hand paddles, support your body in a vertical position in deep water using arm scull only.

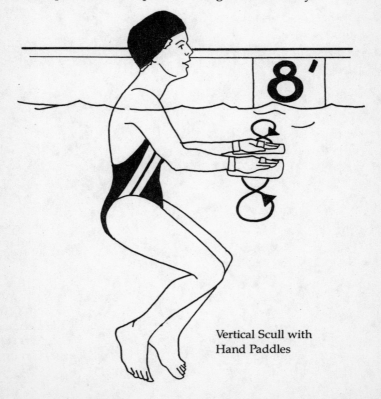

Vertical Scull with
Hand Paddles

Official Individual Medley

In competitive swimming, there is a specific event called the Individual Medley. The following strokes are included in the Individual Medley and are swum in this "official" order: butterfly, backstroke, breaststroke, and freestyle.

W.E.T. Drills
- *Stroke medley:* Standing in chest-deep water, practice arm strokes in the Official Individual Medley order: butterfly, backstroke, breaststroke, freestyle.
- *Kick medley:* Holding on to edge of pool in bracket position, practice kicking in the same official order as the strokes: for butterfly, dolphin kick; for windmill backstroke, back flutter kick; whip kick for breaststroke, and flutter kick for crawl/freestyle.

DAY 29 WORKOUT

Distance: 29 laps (725 yards)
Total Time: 45 minutes

Warm-up with SWEATS to W.E.T.s (5 minutes)

Main Set (35 minutes)

W.E.T. Drills
   Vertical scull
   Stroke medley
   Kick medley

Distance: 29 laps

Laps	1–4	Crawl/freestyle
Laps	5–6	1 lap butterfly and 1 lap backstroke
Laps	7–8	1 lap backstroke and 1 lap breaststroke
Laps	9–10	1 lap breaststroke and 1 lap crawl/freestyle
Laps	11–14	Crawl/freestyle pull with hand paddles
Laps	15–16	Crawl/freestyle—stroke count lower by one
Laps	17–20	Individual Medley—kicking
Laps	21–24	Individual Medley—pulling
Laps	25–28	Individual Medley—swimming
Lap	29	Crawl/freestyle with hand paddles

Cool-down with SWEATS to W.E.T.s (5 minutes)

SWIM TIP: The Individual Medley includes all the competitive swim strokes. You can add variety to your workouts by incorporating a variety of strokes.

LEVEL 5   **DAY 30**

SKILLS: Even-paced Swimming
           Timed Swims, 1, 2, 3 laps

Even-paced Swimming

Even-paced swimming means budgeting your energy over the distance of your swim.

When swimming a particular distance, try to moderate your pace and keep your speed consistent by being aware of your perceived energy exertion. Feel like you're starting very slowly and continue to apply more energy for each lap to maintain a consistent pace throughout your swim.

W.E.T. Drill

• *Progressive S-pull pattern*: Stand in shallow water and do "S" stroke slowly for 10 pulls. Continue to apply slight pressure for next 10 pulls and finish with 10 energetic pulls. Rest and repeat with each stroke in Individual Medley order.

DAY 30 WORKOUT

Distance: 30 laps (750 yards)
Total Time: 45 minutes

Warm-up with SWEATS to W.E.T.s (5 minutes)

Main Set (35 minutes)

W.E.T. Drills
Progressive S-pull pattern
Medley of kicks
Medley of pulls

Distance: 750 yards

Laps 1–20	Crawl/freestyle: To maintain an even pace, begin slowly and very gradually increase intensity
Laps 21–24	Individual Medley
Lap 25	1 lap-timed swim (swim at comfortable pace you could maintain for 3–4 laps)
	Rest
Laps 26–27	2 lap-timed swim
	Rest
Laps 28–30	3 lap-timed swim
	Record your times for the above swims on Appendix C

Optional timed swim

4 laps	Crawl/freestyle
	This brings your 4-lap swim distance to 850 yards or approximately ½ mile.

Cool-down with SWEATS to W.E.T.s (5 minutes)

SWIM TIP: In a timed swim, you should have a particular goal or speed you wish to achieve. In order to swim your best times, you need to constantly hold your pace by starting more slowly than you think you need to and build as you continue. Otherwise you may swim too fast, too hard, and too soon. Follow your workout and you'll have a great swim!

AND BEYOND: THE MAGIC MILE

Congratulations! You've mastered the basic swim techniques competitive swimmers use. But your best bonus, as you have probably
noticed, is your increased fitness, well-being, and enjoyment.

Now that swimming the *30 Laps in 30 Days* program is a piece of
cake, you might wonder: Is there life beyond 30 laps? Of course! Your
swimming goals can continually be challenged. In fact, you might go
for the "Big One," that is, the Magic Mile!

A Note About Workout Notation

As you increase your laps to reach the one-mile distance, there are
new ways of notating your laps for your workout.

Examples: One lap in a 25-yard pool:
   1×25 yards = 1 lap total (25 yards swum once) ($1 \times 1 = 1$ lap)
   4×25 yards = 4 lap swim ($4 \times 1 = 4$ laps)
   1×100 yards = 4 laps swum consecutively ($1 \times 4 = 4$ laps)
   2×100 yards = 4 laps swum consecutively twice ($2 \times 4 = 8$ laps)

Since the number of laps continues to increase, you may wish to
incorporate this notation for your workouts, and continue to count the
total number of laps. Although these workouts are for a 25-yard pool,
the notation used can be adapted for a pool of any length.

The following sample "main set" workouts from days 31–40 will
help you to reach your goal by gradually increasing your laps and
distance to the "Magic Mile."

Main Sets: Reaching the Magic Mile

Day 31   1000 yards (40 laps)

1×400 yards (16 laps)	Crawl/freestyle
1×300 yards (12 laps)	Pull
1×200 yards (8 laps)	Kick
1×100 yards (4 laps)	Individual Medley

Day 32   1200 yards (48 laps)

1×600 yards (24 laps)	Every third lap, favorite stroke
1×400 yards (16 laps)	Every fourth lap, weakest stroke
1×200 yards (8 laps)	Individual Medley

Day 33   1400 yards (56 laps)

4 × 200 yards (4 × 8 laps = 32 total laps)   Crawl/ freestyle
4 × 100 yards (4 × 4 laps = 16 total laps)   Individual Medley
4 ×   50 yards (4 × 2 laps =   8 total laps)   Stroke choice

Day 34   1500 yards (60 laps)

1 × 500 yards (20 laps)   Crawl/freestyle
1 × 400 yards (16 laps)   Pull medley
1 × 300 yards (12 laps)   Kick medley
1 × 200 yards (8 laps)   Breaststroke/Backstroke
1 × 100 yards (4 laps)   Individual Medley

Day 35   1600 yards (64 laps)

4 × 400 yards (4 × 16 = 64 laps)
1 × 400 (16 laps)   Crawl/freestyle
1 × 400 (16 laps)   Alternating free-backstroke
1 × 400 (16 laps)   Every third lap kick on back
1 × 400 (16 laps)   Rest 30 seconds after every four laps

DAY 36   1650 yards (66 laps)

This is a descending set of laps. Begin with 11 laps, resting briefly, and then lower your lap count by one, e.g., 10 laps. Then rest and swim nine laps, etc., down to one lap. Crawl/freestyle or stroke choice.

11 laps	(1 × 275 yards)
10 laps	(1 × 250 yards)
9 laps	(1 × 225 yards)
8 laps	(1 × 200 yards)
7 laps	(1 × 175 yards)
6 laps	(1 × 150 yards)
5 laps	(1 × 125 yards)
4 laps	(1 × 100 yards)
3 laps	(1 × 75 yards)
2 laps	(1 × 50 yards)
1 laps	(1 × 25 yards)
66 laps	1650 yards

Day 37   1800 yards (72 laps) = approx. 1 mile

Alternate each swim with crawl/freestyle and your stroke choice.

$$2 \times 25 \ (2 \times 1 \text{ lap} \ = 2 \text{ laps})$$
$$2 \times 50 \ (2 \times 2 \text{ laps} = 4 \text{ laps})$$
$$2 \times 75 \ (2 \times 3 \text{ laps} = 6 \text{ laps})$$
$$2 \times 100 \ (2 \times 4 \text{ laps} = 8 \text{ laps})$$
$$2 \times 125 \ (2 \times 5 \text{ laps} = 10 \text{ laps})$$
$$2 \times 150 \ (2 \times 6 \text{ laps} = 12 \text{ laps})$$
$$2 \times 175 \ (2 \times 7 \text{ laps} = 14 \text{ laps})$$
$$2 \times 200 \ (2 \times 8 \text{ laps} = 16 \text{ laps})$$

Day 38   1800 yards (72 laps) = approx. 1 mile

Divide your mile into thirds

1 × 600 (24 laps)	Swim
1 × 600 (24 laps)	Pull
1 × 600 (24 laps)	Kick

Day 39   1800 yards (72 laps) = approx. 1 mile

Divide your mile in half
(Try to pace each ½ mile evenly)

1 × 900 yards (36 laps)	Time _____
1 × 900 yards (36 laps)	Time _____

Day 40   1760 yards (70.4 laps) = Exactly 1 mile

1 × 1760 yards (70.4 laps)
GO FOR IT! SWIM A STRAIGHT MILE!

Use "Your Own Workout" chart on page 138 to create your own workout.

CHAPTER ~ 3

Ask Dr. Jane: Common Questions and Concerns

Q: *This is the first time I've used water exercise in a structured way. Are there any guidelines you can give me?*

A: First, you should do W.E.T.s in a comfortable water temperature which is in the low to mid 80s (degrees Fahrenheit). You should exercise in chin- to chest-deep water for best water resistance. While you exercise you should breathe fully and continuously and when you can, exercise to music you enjoy. You can add equipment for greater resistance against the water. For company, invite a friend, a date or a mate, or family member. This can be a wonderful family affair.

Here's a guide to estimating the number of laps no matter where you swim.

Lap Guideline Chart

	Length in Feet	Length in Yards	Approximate No. of Laps Per 100 Yards
	37.5	12.5	8
	60	20	5
Standard	75	25	4
	100	33	3
	165 (50 meters) (Olympic size)	55	2

123

Q: *If I cannot get to the pool, how can I practice my swim skills?*

A: Whether you are at home, at work, or traveling, take a few minutes to do any or all of the following W.E.T.s back to SWEATS—water exercises done on terra firma.

Lower Body: While seated on a straight chair, on the edge of a sofa or a bed, find a comfortable way to practice:

- The flutter kick for your crawl and windmill backstroke
- Modified whip kick for the elementary backstroke
- Dolphin kick for the butterfly

Upper Body: While sitting at your desk, or at a table, or watching TV, practice the following upper body exercises:

- Overarm stretch
- Triceps stretch
- Head and shoulder rolls

Mirror Watch: You can be a self-critic by standing or sitting in front of a full-length mirror and simulating the arm movements for all the strokes. You get immediate feedback because mirrors don't lie!

For the crawl stroke, place a straight-backed chair in front of you and use its width to keep your arms shoulder width apart as you practice the crawl arm stroke.

You can even perfect your rhythmic breathing without having to be in the pool. Fill a basin, a bowl, a pot, a wok, or the bathroom sink with enough lukewarm water so that you can comfortably immerse your face up to your hairline. Exhale into the water through your nose and mouth, forming bubbles. Then turn your head to your breathing side to inhale, and once again exhale into the water. You are doing your rhythmic breathing as if you were swimming.

For breaststroke and butterfly breathing, practice lifting and lowering your chin just above the water, exhaling as you lower your face into the water, forming bubbles, and inhaling as you lift up your head.

I suggest you make a regular practice of doing those SWEATS to W.E.T.s, especially on days between your swims. You will be reinforcing your swim skills and keeping yourself toned, fit and eager to get to your next swim workout.

Q: *How should I adapt my eating schedule to the time of day I swim?*

A: *Sunrise swimmer.* If you do an "early-bird" workout, have a light breakfast, perhaps consisting of two portions of carbohydrates, before you swim.

Liquid luncher. If you have an opportunity to swim during your lunch break, but no chance to "snack," have a substantial breakfast, e.g., two or three portions from starch foods, one protein, and one fruit.

Pre-din swimmer. If you swim before dinner, but have no opportunity for an after-lunch snack, have both a substantial breakfast and lunch each with at least two starches and one protein.

Post-din swimmer. If you swim after your evening meal, have a substantial breakfast, lunch, and snacks so that your "supper" can be reasonably light.

Q: *Why do I always drink a lot of water after swimming, after all, I've been in water during my workout.*

A: Even though swimming feels like a "no sweat" activity, you actually do perspire, and you are dehydrating. So be sure you take an H_2O break before and after your swim. And even during your swim, drink water!

Q: *What should I do about remembering my lock combination?*

A: Forgetting or confusing the numbers of your lock combination does happen. You can cure that by using a ballpoint pen and writing the combination on the inside of your goggle strap or on the inside of your bathing cap, or on the tag inside your swimsuit. But don't leave home without it!

Q: *Is it possible to alter the proportions of my body through this program?*

A: It is very difficult to change one's body proportions; they are your birthright.

What you can do is work toward a redistribution of your body weight.

Understand, too, that exercise may increase your body weight at the same time it decreases the amount of fat you carry because muscle weighs more than fat. You will look trimmer even though there may not be an appreciable difference in your weight.

This swim program, done consistently and in conjunction with a sensible eating regimen, will help you burn up fat, build muscle tone and affect weight loss.

Q: *I do a swim workout regularly, but am planning to become pregnant soon. Should I continue to swim during my pregnancy?*

A: After obtaining your doctor's approval, continue swimming regularly but avoid overexertion. This program, which combines laps and water exercises, will help make your pregnancy more comfortable and enjoyable. It will keep your muscles supple and strong, helping prepare you for labor and delivery.

Q: *I have arthritis. Should I follow your program?*

A: Absolutely! First, see your doctor before beginning. With your physician's OK, slowly start with the SWEATS to W.E.T.s warm-up/cool-down exercises. They will gently stretch your muscles and increase circulation to your joints. In the water, there is almost no impact on stressed areas of your body. Move on to laps when you are comfortable and ready.

Q: *I have a back problem. What swim skills and strokes are best for me?*

A: The backstroke, both elementary and windmill, are most effective for back concerns. They allow a comfortable position to be maintained for back support. You might also try the sidestroke. Avoid the butterfly stroke entirely. Check with your doctor periodically.

Q: *I am a senior with a cardiac condition. How can I follow your program?*

A: You can follow this program, after checking with your doctor, by slowly beginning with SWEATS to W.E.T.s—especially water walking. Then gradually increase your workout to include laps.

Q: *I occasionally have shoulder and/or leg problems. How can I continue my program?*

A: If your upper body area, for instance, your shoulders, is giving you difficulty, concentrate on lower body skills and W.E.T.s exercises, e.g., kicking while sitting on the edge of the pool, or using a kickboard on which to rest your arms and shoulders while kicking laps.

If your lower body, say, your knees, are bothering you, practice your upper body arm skills and W.E.T.s using a pull-buoy to support the legs.

Q: *Sometimes I get a cramp. How can I avoid it?*

A: Most often a cramp occurs because you are kicking too hard, or when you have not done a warm-up. A leg cramp occurs most often in the calf muscle. If you feel a cramp coming on, stop at once and release the contracting fibers by applying direct pressure with your fist to the affected area, and quickly release. Repeat until you feel more comfortable.

Q: *I know I'm not in shape, but I get winded very fast when I swim. Am I doing something wrong?*

A: First, you should warm up for at least five minutes. Also, a lot of people who are just beginning to swim seriously tend to over-kick, that is, try to get more propulsion from their leg movement than proper swimming is designed to provide. If you are over-kicking, the large muscles in your legs are using up a lot of oxygen, therefore, you feel exhausted quickly. Since most swim strokes are done from your upper body, concentrate on getting your speed from your arms and shoulders and train your legs to do less, especially with crawl/freestyle.

Q: *How can I apply W.E.T.s to the skills of other sports I enjoy?*

A: W.E.T.s can be used to "cross-train" for specific movements of other sports as well as to strengthen and condition your muscles, especially when you're not participating in other seasonal activities. In this way using W.E.T.s allows you to maintain and improve those other sports skills so that you're ready to participate when the season arrives and so avoid possible injury. The "aqua jog" and "stroke punch" are sample W.E.T.s which can be used for that purpose. For example, for arm activities such as tennis, baseball, and golf, you can use hand paddles or a pull-buoy for extra resistance in the water. For walking, jogging, cross-country skiing, and downhill skiing, which are alternating arm and leg movements, you can simulate these motions against the water's resistance.

Q: *I am interested in becoming a competitive swimmer and may also want to enter a triathlon. How can I prepare myself?*

A: If the smell of chlorine and the roar of the crowd whets your appetite, go for the swimmers' endorphin high. Check with your local swim facility as to what swim clubs exist in your area which schedule workouts. You may want to also consider Masters Swimming. This is a competitive program for adults from ages 25 to 90 in five-year age groups. Meets are held locally, regionally, nationally and internationally. For more information in your local area, contact United States Masters Swimming. See Appendix A for specific information regarding competitive and other aquatic organizations.

Q: *I get to a certain point in the program and cannot make progress. What should I do?*

A: What you need is a pep talk, so here it is. You should view hitting a "plateau" as part of a bigger picture of swimming for fitness, with all the long-term benefits that interested you initially. There's a dedication and self-discipline that goes with any long-term goal; time and energy are required to see the progress you want, especially if you want to go a long way with it.

Good swimmers aren't born; they're made! Stay with your program!

Q: *How can I be prepared for a safe swim?*

A: Never swim alone. Be sure a lifeguard is present on deck. Listen to your body! Do your warm-up and cool-down! Learn the ABCs of CPR (Cardio-Pulmonary Resuscitation). Call your local American Heart Association or Red Cross chapter for courses near you.

Q: *Sometimes I think swimming is a contact sport. What are the rules of the pool?*

A: Courtesy does count! The recent surge in fitness swimming has intensified the need for observing procedures of poolside courtesy, especially since pools and rules are not always created equal with regard to lap length, speed, number of swimmers per lane and allotted time per swim session.

Review the following swimming courtesy guidelines for your swim facility:

- Lanes in pools are often divided by speed. Start "modestly." Speed is relative to which lane you are in and with whom you're swimming.
- Observe the posted swimming patterns in your facility. Where there are two swimmers allowed in a lane, they usually split the lane.
- If you are circle swimming, you will always be swimming on the right-hand side of the lane and moving in a counterclockwise direction.
- To pass a slower swimmer, first tap the toes of that swimmer. Then, when you reach the wall, make your turn and precede the slower swimmer.
- Use equipment courteously. Avoid hanging on to lane lines, blocking the pace clock, or interfering with lap swimmers by standing at the shallow end of the lane.

If there are differences of opinion between swimmers, the lifeguard should be immediately consulted.

WRAP-UP

I hope you have learned through *Swim 30 Laps in 30 Days* that swimming is technical as well as fun; that there is a structure to a stroke; that how to breathe while swimming is not a mystery.

I also hope new swimmers are now competent swimmers and previously accomplished swimmers have improved stroke technique and lap distance and time.

You have prepared yourself for the future in fitness and good health. Swimming and water exercise are moving happily along into the 21st century, becoming *the* fitness programs of choice among people of all ages and abilities, as well as benefiting those with special needs.

Best of all, swimming is a family affair—and it's for a lifetime! See you poolside.

———Jane Katz

A P P E N D I X ~ A

Aquatic Organizations and Sources

For more information contact the following organizations and sources:

AEA   Aquatic Exercise Association
P.O. Box 497
Port Washington, WI 53074
(414) 284-3416

ANRC   American National Red Cross
17th and D Streets NW
Washington, DC 20006
(202) 737-8300

AF   Arthritis Foundation
1314 Spring Street, NW
Atlanta, GA 30309
(404) 872-7100

ISHOF   International Swimming Hall of Fame
1 Hall of Fame Drive
Fort Lauderdale, FL 33316
(305) 462-6536

NSPI   National Spa and Pool Institute
2111 Eisenhower Avenue
Alexander, VA 22314
(703) 838-0083

PCPFS   President's Council on Physical Fitness and Sports
450 Fifth Street NW
Washington, DC 20001
(202) 272-3421

USOA   Underwater Society of America
Fin Swimming
PO Box 628
Daly City, CA 94017
(415) 583-8492

USMS	United States Masters Swimming 2 Peters Avenue Rutland, MA 01549 (508) 886-6631
USSI	United States Swimming, Inc. 1750 Boulder Street Colorado Spring, CO 80909 (303) 578-4578
USSSI	United States Synchronized Swimming Inc. Pan Am Plaza Suite 510 201 S. Capitol Street Indianapolis, IN 46225 (317) 237-5700
USWFA	United States Water Fitness Association PO Box 3601333 Boynton Beach, FL 33436 (407) 732-9908
YMCA of the USA	"Y" USA 101 N. Wacker Drive Chicago, IL 60606 (312) 977-0031 1-800-USA-YMCA

Magazines for Fitness and Masters Swimmers

Aquatics Magazine
6255 Barfield Road
Atlanta, GA 30328

Fitness Swimmer
318 E. 39th Street
New York, NY 10016–2106

Swim Magazine
P.O. Box 45497
Los Angeles, CA 90045

The following is a selection of aquatic equipment companies for your swim gear and accessories.

Arena USA
28 Engelhard Drive
Cranbury, NJ 08512
(609) 655-1515

Gulbenkian Swimwear
7 Memorial Park Plaza
Pleasantville, NY 10570
(914) 747-3240
1-800-431-2586

The Finals
21 Minisink Avenue
Port Jervis, NY 12771
1-800-431-9111

Hind
P.O. Box 12609
San Luis Obispo, CA 93406
1-800-235-4150

Ocean Pool Company
45 Mall Drive
Commack, NY 11725
(516) 543–1110
1-800-645-5316

Speedo America
7915 Haskell Avenue
Van Nuys, CA 91409
1-800-547-8770

TYR Sport
PO Box 1007
Huntington Beach, CA 92647
(714) 897-0799

The Victor
2725 W. 81st Street
Hialeah, FL 33016
1-800-356-5132

A P P E N D I X ~ B

Stroke Checklist Charts

Checklist for Crawl/Freestyle

If You Are Doing This . . .

Try This . . .

1. Lifting head out of the water for breath to one or both sides (Coney Island swimmer).

1. At home practice rhythmic breathing. Turn head to one side only. In the water, keep your ear on the surface of the water as you turn for a breath.

2. Hands enter and arms pull across midline of body.

2. Hold kickboard widthwise with arms at ends and practice stroking, shoulder-width apart.

3. Kick too high and hard above surface, splashing water.

3. Just make water "boil." Use wall, kickboard and/or fins for practice. Try a crossover kick.

4. Covering too little distance for perceived energy exertion.

4. Practice the S-shaped pull with body roll. During your workout, focus on your crawl/freestyle drills.

Comparison Chart

	Crawl	Freestyle
Breathing	Rhythmic breathing	Rhythmic breathing Alternate breathing
Pulling	Straight arm pull	S-shaped pull
Body Rotation	Minimal body rotation	Body rotation up to 45 degrees
Kicking	Flutter kick	Crossover kick

Checklist for Elementary Backstroke

If You Are Doing This . . .

1. No glide after each stroke.

2. Arms splash when pulling and/or recovering above water.

3. Legs break surface water.

Try This . . .

1. Count for three seconds before starting next stroke cycle. Place greater emphasis on pull phase of arms and whip of legs as they press together.

2. Keep arms underwater throughout stroke. During recovery keep hands close to body. During pull extend arms outward in a comfortable position, depending on your flexibility.

3. Flex feet as knees bend, and drop heels to bottom of the pool. Practice kicking on wall so you can watch your feet.

Checklist for Windmill Backstroke

If You Are Doing This . . .

1. Body position bent at hips, and low in the water.

2. Ankles are stiff, feet are flexed and toes turned outward.

3. Arms bent on recovery.

4. Not covering enough distance per stroke.

Try This . . .

1. Streamline the body position by keeping head back while back is arched slightly, pushing hips up, squeezing buttocks.

2. Turn feet inward with big toes pointed brushing past each other. Use fins to improve ankle flexibility.

3. Keep elbows straight as arms recover and hand first enters overhead.

4. Use the bent-arm "S" pull and roll your shoulders which allows you to pull more efficiently.

Checklist for Breaststroke

If You Are Doing This . . .

1. Pull too wide beyond shoulders and body is low in the water.

2. Lift head for breath after you pull.

3. Rely on arms for most propulsion since kick lacks power.

4. Arms feel slow or sluggish.

Try This . . .

1. Keep your hands in sight throughout the pull and recovery, and do not allow hands to pull past your shoulders.

2. Lift head at the start of the heart-shaped pull (catch) as forearms press outward as well as slightly downward. Head will lift as shoulders rise up naturally.

3. Flex feet and raise heels toward buttocks at hip width for propulsion of whip kick. Practice in bracket position facing wall.

4. Recover your arms quickly by squeezing elbows and forearms together to a prayer position and immediately extending arms forward.

Checklist for Sidestroke

If You Are Doing This . . .

1. Continual movement of arms and legs with head too high and legs too low.

2. Legs splash water.

3. Leg kick more a hindrance than a support.

Try This . . .

1. Count to 3 between stroke cycles to streamline body. Keep your ear in the water.

2. Stabilize body on side (rather than on front or back). Use kickboard under bottom arm for support.

3. Flex foot of forward leg to catch water. Foot of back leg is pointed. Use kickboards under each arm for support to practice scissor kick.

Checklist for Butterfly

If You Are Doing This . . .

Try This . . .

1. Head stays up too long during breath inhalation.

1. Nod head forward in water after inhalation to allow arms to recover easily. Exhale air underwater.

2. Arms recover below water surface.

2. Keep elbows higher than your hand. Stretch out with SWEATS to W.E.T.s to improve flexibility.

3. Knees bend excessively, with feet breaking surface of the water.

3. Practice body wave W.E.T. drill to improve hip undulation. When swimming, kick downward forcefully and relax your feet during the upbeat of the kick.

4. "Slipping" through the water— not covering enough distance per stroke, with body and hips low.

4. Concentrate on keyhole arm pattern and undulating of hips.

Stroke Reference Chart

This chart highlights the strokes and techniques described in this book. It can be used as a quick reference illustrating what kick to use with what arm pull. In addition, a suggested "swim quotient" or ratio of kicking power to arm-pulling power in each of the strokes is indicated.

Pattern	Stroke	Arms	Legs	Percent of Stroke's Power From Arms	Percent of Stroke's Power From Legs
Alternating	Crawl	Straight arm pull	Flutter kick	60	40
	Freestyle	S-shaped pull	Crossover kick	80	20
	Windmill backstroke	Straight arm pull	Flutter kick	65	35
	Backstroke	Bent-arm pull	Flutter kick	75	25
Simultaneous	Elementary backstroke	"V" pull	Whip or frog kick	50	50
	Breaststroke	Heart-shaped pull	Whip or frog kick	50	50
	Butterfly	Keyhole pull	Dolphin kick—1 or 2 beats	65	35
Asymmetrical Variation	Sidestroke	Regular "accordion" pull	Scissor kick, regular or inverted	50	50

A P P E N D I X ~ D

Progress Charts

Timed Swims Progress Chart

Level	Day	Place/Date	Distance	Time	Pulse Check	Comments
1	3		1 lap/ 25 yds			
	6		1 lap/ 25 yds			
2	9		1 lap/ 25 yds			
	12		2 laps/ 50 yds			
3	15		2 laps/ 50 yds			
	18		2 laps/ 50 yds			
4	21		3 laps/ 75 yds			
	24		3 laps/ 75 yds			
5	27		3 laps/ 75 yds			
	30		1 lap			
			2 laps			
			3 laps			
			4 laps			

Your Own Workout Chart

Warm-up (SWEATS to W.E.T.s)
(5 minutes)

_____

_____

_____

_____

Main Set (15–35 minutes)
　　W.E.T Drills

_____

_____

_____

_____

　　Distance (in laps)

_____

_____

_____

_____

_____

　　Timed swim and pulse check_____

Cool-down (SWEATS to W.E.T.s)
(5 minutes)

_____

_____

_____

_____

Your Personal Swim Log

Level 1: Crawl Stroke

Day	Dates	Total Laps	Total Time	Pulse Check	Swim Skills Checklist	Comments
1					Breathing Face float, glide, and recovery Flutter kick	
2					Crawl arm stroke Crawl arm stroke with flutter kick Rhythmic breathing Rhythmic breathing with arm stroke	
3					Crawl stroke Reading the clock 1 lap	
4					Open turn	
5					Splashback Arm stroke	
6					Wide hand entry High elbow recovery Timed swim and pulse check 1 lap	

Your Personal Swim Log

Level 2: Backstroke

Day	Dates	Total Laps	Total Time	Pulse Check	Swim Skills Checklist	Comments
7					Back float and recovery Back glide and flutter kick	
8					Treading	
9					Back sculling Timed swim and pulse check 1 lap	
10					Elementary backstroke arm motion Closed turn	
11					Whip kick Elementary backstroke	
12					Windmill backstroke Timed swim and pulse check 2 laps	

Your Personal Swim Log

Level 3: Breaststroke and Freestyle

Day	Dates	Total Laps	Total Time	Pulse Check	Swim Skills Checklist	Comments
13					Breaststroke arm motion	
14					Whip kick Breaststroke	
15					"S" pull Timed swim 2 laps	
16					Freestyle body roll Continuous swim 8 laps	
17					Crossover kick	
18					Windmill backstroke with "S" pull Timed swim 2 laps	

141

Your Personal Swim Log

Level 4: Sidestroke

Day	Dates	Total Laps	Total Time	Pulse Check	Swim Skills Checklist	Comments
19					Sidestroke arm motion Continuous swim 10 laps	
20					Scissor kick Sidestroke	
21					Kickboard skills Timed swim 3 laps	
22					Face front sculling Easy/brisk pace	
23					Stroke count Number of strokes per lap	
24					Turns and push-offs Quick lightning turn Timed swim 3 laps	

Your Personal Swim Log

Level 5: Butterfly

Day	Dates	Total Laps	Total Time	Pulse Check	Swim Skills Checklist	Comments
25					Butterfly arm motion Timed rest intervals	
26					Dolphin kick Butterfly stroke Single beat kick	
27					Alternate breathing for crawl/freestyle Butterfly Timed swim 3 laps	
28					Flip turn Speed variations	
29					Sculling with hand paddles Official Individual Medley	
30					Even-paced swimming Timed swims 1, 2, 3 laps	

About the Author

Though born in Sharon, Pennsylvania, Jane Katz, Ed.D., is otherwise a native New Yorker. She attended its schools and swam in its public pools. She earned her doctor of education in gerontology at Columbia University.

She was a member at age 13 of the American Swim Team to the Maccabiah Games. As a member of the 1964 United States Performance Team in Tokyo, Japan, Dr. Katz helped pioneer the acceptance of synchronized swimming as an Olympic event.

Her achievements as a Master's long-distance, competitive, synchronized, and fin swimmer have earned her National, All-American, and International Championships. She has been recognized for her work as an educator, physical fitness innovator, and author. Among many prestigious honors for her work is the Townsend Harris Academic Medal from City College, which puts her in the company of fellow alumni recipients General Colin Powell and Dr. Jonas Salk.

She is a water safety instructor trainer for the American National Red Cross, she has been a consultant to the President's Council on Physical Fitness and Sports, and she received the Healthy American Fitness Leaders Award from the President's Council. Recently, Dr. Katz was appointed by the International Swimming Hall of Fame to serve on its board of directors.

Through her clinics and demonstrations, as well as TV appearances, Dr. Katz has been able to reach virtually everyone from the novice water exerciser to the experienced swimmer.

As a professor of health and physical education in the City University of New York (CUNY), Dr. Katz has taught thousands of people from all ethnic backgrounds, skills, and ages who have attended Bronx Community College and John Jay College of Criminal Justice to swim farther, faster, and better.